Jewish U

A Contemporary Guide for the Jewish College Student

Scott Aaron

Foreword by
Richard M. Joel

UAHC Press
New York, New York

Library of Congress Cataloging-in-Publication Data

Aaron, Scott.
    Jewish U: a contemporary guide for the Jewish college student / Scott Aaron.
        p. cm.
    Includes bibliographical references (p.) and appendix.
    ISBN 0-8074-0790-9
        1. Jewish college students—United States.   2. College student orientation—United States.
    3. Jewish way of life. I. Title.

LB3613.J4 A37 2002
378.1′982992′4—dc21

                                                                    2002024201

Art on page 16 by Melissa Katzman
Designer: Shaul Akri
Typesetting: El Ot Ltd., Tel Aviv
This book is printed on acid-free paper.
Copyright © 2002 by Scott Aaron
Manufactured in the United States of America
10 9 8 7 6 5 4 3

To my parents for nurturing my boyhood,

to my wife Donni for partnering with me in adulthood,

to my sons Meitav and Nitzan for the adventure and joy of parenthood,

and to all of my college students who have taught me about life

what no one else could.

You have all taught me something, and today I call you all Rabbi.

Contents

Spring Semester

Foreword

Jewishness is a funny thing: it works, or doesn't, on an individual and collective level. One can't speak of a successful Jewish community or a successful Jewish people if "Jewish" is not working for individuals. We are always concerned about *k'lal* and *p'rat,* the general and the specific. While the pages that follow concern themselves with how Jewish students can find their best Jewish journey through college, we can also see in them a prescription for rebuilding the Jewish people.

We have reached a point in our history that could be plagiarized as "the best of times and the worst of times." Jews have never been more accepted, more welcomed, or more successful in a society as we are today in America. And, if we are not mindful, the price of that success could be our disappearance. Since we are at home here in America, and the dream is ours to share, our challenge is to see whether we dream in Jewish. For generation after generation, there was no discussion of whether we were Jews and would stay Jews. We were society's "other," regardless of the society we were in. Often, we were also defined by our victimhood. Hence, the bittersweet humor of Woody Allen, who would opine that the Jewish definition of swimming is "not drowning."

But today, being Jewish is an option, not a condition. We survive not if we're the chosen people, but if we're the choosing people. And the question we face, that's real, is should we choose Jewish, should we exercise the Jewish option? Many of us believe that we were equipped to die as Jews, but not equipped to live as Jews. Far too many young Jewish people have reached the level of maturity that gets them to college with a profoundly underdeveloped "J" chromosome. Jewish college students are often equipped with a fine twelfth-grade intellectual education and, all too often, with a stunted, unexciting, unintellectual, valueless Jewish exposure. They come to campus equipped to compete and excel at all classes except Jew 101. And they fear that if they enroll in that course, they'll flunk. So they "major" in something else.

So, in a real sense, the experience of campus in the twenty-first century, for a Jew, is not just about the individual—it's about our people. It's not just about Joe and Jane Jew tilling the groves of academe remembering they're Jews; it's about the campus as a model for valuable Jewish communities of passion and purpose that make it a "no-brainer" for young Jews to exercise the Jewish option. Campus can and must be the vanguard of a Jewish renaissance. Our children will choose Jewish if it's a valuable choice. We model what we are supposed to be, what we can be, what we can reach for, as individuals and as a people on campus.

Eighty-five percent of Jews of college age attend college. The overwhelming number of Jewish people of this age cohort are in campus communities with significant Jewish populations. If we can model a language of Jewish value and meaning that works for this group, we will have thousands leaving campus proud to be Jews and seeking to live Jewishly. So these years are not just important for each student. They're critical for the Jewish future. And many of us believe that campus today is a wonderful locale for plotting the Jewish future and for the Jewish people to reassert themselves as valuable partners in an America of values.

The only thing constant on campus is change. And on campus, the times, they are a changin'. The monumental forces of globalization, and the shock of September 11, have created new opportunities to begin discussions about values and truths, about right and wrong, about good and evil. A culture of relativism is being forced to yield to a collective of questioning. Rabbi Adin Steinsaltz has said that Americans are used to confronting danger, but are not used to confronting evil. All of the cataclysm of contemporary life contributes to a feeling among young people of anonymity, of existential loneliness, and of uncertainty. But it also yields to the idealism of youth that insists on mattering, that seeks meaning. Young people want a life that makes sense, a life of worth and meaning. And if the Jewish community is willing to present a Jewishness to its children that is valuable, meaningful, nontrivial, purposeful, and even noble and offer it with the variety that currently exists, campus can be the great galvanizer of Jewish life.

Fortunately, what most students will find on campus is Jewish joy, Jewish pride, Jewish variety, and Jewish opportunity. This guide presents you with a programmatic road map through a Jewish year on campus. While program specifics vary based on the complexion of each campus and the resources available on each campus, the basic principles of Jewish life are more the same than they are different. What is critical is that each student carefully choose the kind of campus that works best for him or her. The choice of the type of Jewish community on campus is as crucial as exploring the choices of majors available. It should be made carefully, with the student and his or her family fully investigating the array of possibilities. Hillels are wonderful partners in helping with that exploration. Regardless of the specifics of your choice, you can expect that all major campuses share basic principles of Jewish community.

Community of Communities. Campus communities today are usually modeled much more on a community model than on a synagogue model. Rather than find an institution or Jewish club on campus, the student can expect to find a community of communities. Most successful Hillels offer an array of Jewish clubs, groupings, or committees that cater to particular needs or interests of students. There will be an array of social, service, educational, spiritual, and Israel opportunities. Professional staff on campus are trained to provide students with quality choices and seek to assist the student in growing Jewishly, in the direction the student wants.

Pluralism. We live in times today where one size of Jewishness does not fit all—one size fits one. Therefore, campuses are geared up to offer multiple opportunities that span the religious streams of the community. There is extant on campus a philosophy of pluralism that proclaims, "Let a thousand Jewish flowers blossom." And while there will be multiple religious opportunities on most campuses that run from the experimental to liberal to conservative, the Jewish community encourages healthy discussion, debate, and diversity, in an environment of respect and esteem. Pluralism today rejects a relativism that proclaims that all ways are right; it embraces the notion that all ways are worthy of respect. A Jewish future will be healthy if we learn that it's all right to disagree profoundly over ideas, but to do it lovingly and within the boundaries of Jewish ideas. A pluralist community is not always a neat community; sometimes there are tensions. But a university community should be one where we model the sanctity of ideas, where we find Jewish themes that unite us, even as we explore ideas that we might debate.

A key challenge is to offer Jewish learning and educational opportunities that do not intimidate students who might not have the background of others, while always offering challenges to students' intellectual potential. These opportunities often exist within the curriculum of the university through Jewish studies and within extra- or co-curricular offerings of Hillel and other organizations. Ideas are supposed to be central to the university, and Jewish ideas should be no less exciting, challenging, and high quality than others.

Empowerment and Engagement.   It is also true that students come to campus with different perspectives on their Jewishness. A minority of Jewish students arrive on campus comfortable with and confident in their Jewishness. These students need to be empowered, to be encouraged to grow and to lead, to build programs and pathways that continue their Jewish growth and enhance their comfort level in valuable Jewish involvements.

The silent majority of Jewish students arrive on campus Jewishly undereducated, undercelebrated, and underexperienced. Jewish life has often not resonated to students outside the home. A majority of students have not been active in high school youth movements, Jewish camping, or day school; most have never visited Israel. But most of these students have not rejected being Jewish—they have simply not seen Jewish life as theirs or as valuable. These students will probably not feel comfortable with normative Jewish programming—they feel they don't own it. However, there is a great opportunity to engage these students—to offer an array of "Jewish doing" opportunities that enable the student to grow Jewishly without an environment of intimidation. They might find their connections through a Jewish *a cappella* group, a Greek-Jewish student council, Jewish studies groups, or a college trip to Israel. Students' Jewish growth curves on campus are varied, and campuses are increasingly offering an array of Jewish activities designed to engage the unengaged, often on a one-to-one basis.

Social Action.   Increasingly, students are attracted to service opportunities, where they get to be serious players at improving the world, while doing so in a Jewish context. Through an array of service opportunities, like Hillel's *Tzedek Hillel*, coupled with relevant Jewish learning, thousands of students assist in literacy programs, participate in voter registration efforts, travel on spring-break programs to work with the underprivileged— truly coming to know the Jewish imperative to advance the well-being of the world.

Israel.   Israel is a critical component of Jewish identity. Both the Jews' historic and philosophic connection to the Jewish homeland and our ties to the State of Israel are central to Jewish development. But students of this generation have none of the memories of Israel that their parents have, and it is imperative to accord them opportunities both to learn about the multifaceted realities of Israel and to visit Israel, as well as to study there. Increased resources are being offered to help the Jewish student know and love Israel, not simply defend Israel. Most campuses offer an array of these opportunities, both on a campus level and on a global level.

To rebuild our people requires a serious commitment to give to young people an ownership interest in their Jewishness.

The mood on campus today is one where a variety of quality opportunities exist, often tailored to a dizzying array of student interests. But with all of these opportunities, it still remains true that the student must decide to participate. With all the quality programs, with all the welcoming efforts of students and professionals, with all the encouragement and prodding of parents, the student must still choose.

That is why, in some ways, the most important contribution that can be made to students is to make them aware of the opportunities to "do Jewish" on campus and help them sense the quality and excitement of Jewish choices before ever becoming an undergraduate. This volume can help acculturate and guide the student on that journey. May it be a joyous one.

Richard M. Joel
President and International Director
Hillel: The Foundation for Jewish Campus Life

Acknowledgments

I would like to thank my Hillel rabbi, Abie Ingber at the University of Cincinnati Hillel, for being a role model of pluralism and creativity for my own personal as well as professional campus Judaism; Rabbi Meir Mitelman of Hofstra University Hillel for showing me how much *naches* there is in working with college students; Dr. Sue Dickman, formerly of the Edgar M. Bronfman Center for Jewish Student Life at New York University, for entrusting and empowering me to lead; Joseph Kohane of the Hillel Foundation at the Ohio State University for his mentorship, magic, and "osmosis"; Rabbis Norman Cohen, Larry Raphael, Zahara Davidowitz-Farkas, and Dr. Sherry Blumberg, for assisting me and encouraging me to stay with my interest in the campus rabbinate and for their work with the Steinhardt Scholars experiment at the Hebrew Union College-Jewish Institute of Religion campus in New York City; Rabbi Mark Goldman and Dr. Meryl Goldman of Cincinnati, who have always been friends, mentors, and role models for me both professionally and personally; Debbi, Allie, and Greg, who have always been there for me; my many rabbinic and programmatic colleagues working at Hillels across the country, from whom I continuously learn and gain inspiration and hope for the future of American Jewry; my colleagues at the Brandeis-Bardin Institute, who work with me to make the Brandeis Collegiate Institute the unique and invaluable resource to Jewish college students that it is; Richard Joel, for caring about this book; and Michael Steinhardt, for investing in my rabbinic education and goal to serve the American Jewish campus community. I would also like to thank my editor at UAHC Press, Rabbi Hara Person, for her commitment and extensive effort on this book as well as her honesty and intellectual integrity, and all of the great folks at UAHC Press who helped to get this book to press, including publisher Ken Gesser, Stuart Benick, Rick Abrams, Liane Broido, Debra Hirsch Corman, and Benjamin David. Additional thanks go to those in the Youth Division of the UAHC who helped get this book off the ground and generously gave feedback at critical stages, namely Rabbi Allan Smith, Rabbi Andrew Davids, and Jenny Small.

Fall
Semester

Awwwwwww, Mom!

Mazal Tov! You are getting ready for college! What an exciting time! New places, new faces, new ideas, new adventures! It is probably a bit stressful too though. After all, you have been in school for twelve years preparing for this event. Ever since you were little, you knew this time was coming, and now here it is. It's natural to have some apprehensions and questions amidst the excitement. Not just you, by the way, but your parents and family too. It's natural for them to be a bit stressed as well. You are about to leave home, which means that you are growing up and becoming an adult. Even if you have older siblings who have already left the nest, your folks and family are still going to have to adjust to you leaving.

It is not unusual for parents to do some different and abnormal things until you actually move to campus, like take long melancholy walks down memory lane with you and remind you of every "adorable" thing you ever did as a child. Or they may become a bit more critical of you and end each disagreement with something like "Do you think you'll get away with that in college?" You may find them suddenly not so sure if they should be telling you what to do as they normally would or wondering about whether you need a curfew anymore. And they may offer you lots of unsolicited advice about what to expect from college and about being on your own. If you received this book as a gift, then someone in your life probably decided you could also use some advice on figuring out what kind of Jew you want to be at college. These behaviors may seem bizarre or even embarrassing now, but it will just take some time for all of you to adjust. After all, these are the people who have cared for you since infancy and who have prepared you for this day when you will leave home. So while all of this strange intimacy is going on, it's also a good time to think about what Jewishly you might want to take with you from your childhood home into your new adulthood.

No, really Grandma, this book is much better than money!—or, So what?

Chances are that if you received this book as a gift, your eyebrows went up a bit. It probably wasn't at the top of your wish list. After all, you are heading off to college. You are probably thinking about what to major in, where you

Lech L'cha:

Preparing to Leave Your Parents' Home

What to pack, who to call, who to see, what to finish, and what to leave unfinished before you leave for college are going to live, who you'll become friends with, who you will date, what kind of fun there is to have on campus. You might have gone to religious school, become bar or bat mitzvah, done the High Holy Day thing, gone to family seders, and of course celebrated Chanukah. Maybe you belonged to a Jewish youth group, went to a Jewish summer camp, or traveled to Israel. Or maybe you haven't done any of these things. Either way, at this moment, being Jewish on campus is probably not the highest thing on your list of concerns right now. This book is about helping you find ways to move it up the priority list—maybe not to the top, but onto the desktop menu at least. You've been Jewish all of your life so far, and you will be Jewish all of your adult life. Just as college is the time when you prepare your mind for the adult world, it's also the right time to prepare your heart and soul for adulthood as well.

Why me? Who is this book for?

The vast majority of incoming Jewish college students in North America are Reform, Conservative, Reconstructionist, or unaffiliated with any denomination. This means that they were not raised to be what could be called strictly or traditionally observant, but attended a Reform, Conservative, or Reconstructionist synagogue for their religious education and observance or grew up not attending any synagogue at all. Of course not everyone fits neatly into denominational categories. Some of these students may have gone to a Jewish community center summer camp or belonged to a community youth group like B'nai Brith Youth Organization, while others may have been actively involved in movement-sponsored youth activities like NFTY, USY, and summer camps. A small percentage of these students attended a Jewish day school as well. Unaffiliated students may also have gone to a Jewish community youth group or camp, but they have had little or no formal synagogue affiliation or education nor have they experienced much Jewishly at home. These Jewish students do not define themselves as traditional, meaning that they do not believe that they are traditionally observant of Jewish law as determined in its strictest forms through only Orthodox rabbis, but rather embrace a Conservative, Reform, or Reconstructionist theology and practice or perhaps a combination of those three. With the exception of a few schools, these Jewish students are currently the dominant Jewish group on American college campuses.

Traditionally observant students tend to seek schools where there are other traditional folks like themselves. This is because they tend to embrace a more ritually observant daily lifestyle, and they need a like-minded community that can support those needs. For instance, they might eat only kosher food, so they need a campus that can provide it for them. They might want to attend daily prayer services, so they need a community that can provide a minyan. They might not be comfortable driving on Shabbat, so they need a campus with a Shabbat community within walking distance for services and meals.

Other Jewish students may observe a more flexible but equally meaningful style of Jewish observance, so their options in choosing campuses are more open. These students may choose a campus with a significant Jewish community, but not necessarily a traditionally religious one, because they wish to be able to express their Judaism more socially and culturally. Some may even choose to attend campuses with little to no Jewish campus life. This does not mean that they do not feel Jewishly connected, just that they do not feel the need to seek out a Jewish community in their educational environment.

Does any of this sound familiar to you? If so, this book is for you. While this book touches on issues related to traditional observance, this is not a book about being a traditionally observant Jew on campus.

Take a moment and ask yourself what your thoughts are on being a Jewish college student. How important is it for you to be a part of a Jewish community in college? How are you making that decision? What do you know about the Jewish community on your chosen campus? Have you asked anyone at the school about it? Did you visit the Hillel or Jewish student union when you went on your campus tour? Do you know if any of the various movement-affiliated college groups are represented on campus? If you have not explored this aspect of campus life, it may be worth doing so before you go. Even if you have no interest right now in being Jewishly involved or identified, just find out some basic details in case you ever need to know. As time goes by, you may surprise yourself by feeling the need to get in touch with other Jews on your campus.

Have Torah, will travel!

One of the most fascinating things about Judaism is the portability of our religion and culture. We can literally carry almost everything we need to be Jewishly connected in the trunk of our car! This is because Jews have historically been a transient people. We have wandered the world for centuries, often having to leave what had been a safe and secure home on

A minyan is a prayer group with a minimum of ten people. The minyan represents the local Jewish community as a whole, and certain prayers are traditionally only recited aloud when there is at least a minyan present. Traditional Jews require ten men for a minyan, while other Jews count both men and women for a minyan.

Hillels are Jewish student organizations for college students located on campuses all over North America. Many have their own student center buildings that serve as a resource and programming place for Jewish students. Those without buildings of their own have events and programs in various locations around campus. As their own website says, "Hillel's mission is to maximize the number of Jews doing Jewish with other Jews." Hillel tries to enable Jewish students to find ways to engage in their own way with Judaism and with other Jews. The range of Hillel activities includes community service projects, the arts, social events, holiday observances, learning opportunities, and prayer services. Hillel is open to any student and embraces Jews of all kinds. For more information on Hillel or to find a Hillel on a specific campus, go to http://www.hillel.org.

The following are some of the Jewish student organizations:

- Kesher is part of the Reform Movement. It is the college education department of the Union of American Hebrew Congregations. For more information, go to http://www.keshernet.com or e-mail at Kesher@uahc.org.
- Koach is the college-outreach branch of the Conservative/ Masorti Movement, the United Synagogue of Conservative Judaism. For more information, go to http://www.koach.org.
- Kedma is an international student organization for the Orthodox Movement. For more information, go to http://www.kedma.org or e-mail at Kedma@netscape.net.
- For resources or information related to the Reconstructionist Movement, go to www.jrf.org.

An easy way to get the 411 on your campus's Jewish community is to surf onto the campus profile section of www.hillel.org. If your school is not listed there with information or a link to a campus Jewish website, then just call your campus's office of student affairs and ask for information on religious life on campus. If no one in student affairs knows about Jewish life on campus, then there may not be much to know about. Go back to the Hillel website and contact the Hillel at the closest listed campus to yours. They should be able to tell you what, if anything, is available at your campus.

little notice. We therefore became adept at developing rituals and cultures that could travel with us. College students are also a transient lot, often moving to a different living space each year and usually owning little beyond the clothes and personal possessions that they bring to school with them. As you pack for school, you probably are referring to a list of items the school suggests for incoming students. You may also be getting packing advice from siblings, friends, and other folks who have already been to college. However, you probably have not gotten much advice on what Jewish things you should pack for the big move, so here is a short list of items that you might be glad to have one day in the future.

This list is flexible and should be personalized according to your individual needs. All of the items you bring should reflect your own personal family practice and history. The appropriate use of all of these items will be covered in later chapters in this book.

- Personal prayer items. Chances are that you will be at school for at least one important holiday each year where you will be glad you have these things, not to mention perhaps on a Shabbat or two. They can be items that you use personally or have used in the past, or they can be items given or left to you by family that you cherish even if you don't use them regularly. These might include a *kippah (yarmulke),* a *tallit,* or *t'fillin.*
- Keepsakes and mementos. Think about taking a Star of David or other piece of Jewish jewelry that gives you a good feeling when you are wearing it. Items like these can go far in helping you feel at home in a new environment.
- Your own prayerbook. Perhaps you were given a prayerbook at your bat or bar mitzvah or confirmation. Perhaps your home congregation has its own prayerbook. Either way, while you're away at school you might appreciate having a prayerbook you're comfortable and familiar with. If you don't already own one, the rabbi, cantor, or educator of your home congregation can help you obtain a prayerbook.
- A Jewish calendar. You can get these from your synagogue or campus Hillel usually for free or even on-line with a quick search for "Jewish calendar."
- Ritual items for special celebrations. These include a *Kiddush* cup, candlesticks, a challah cover, seder plate, and *chanukiyah* (Chanukah menorah). You may be surprised at how meaningful and useful these items can be even if you live in a dorm.

1

- A mezuzah from home or a new one especially for your room door. (See chapter 2 for how to hang it.)
- A copy of the Torah or *Tanach.* The *Tanach,* the Jewish Bible, contains only the Torah (the Five Books of Moses) and two other sections—*N'vi-im,* Prophets, and *K'tuvim,* Writings. Bibles that include the New Testament are not Jewish bibles.
- A *bencher,* a small book of traditional home rituals and songs that are sung on Shabbat and holidays.
- If you play an instrument like the guitar, or just like to sing, there are many collections of Jewish music that you can play when the mood strikes you.
- A *tzedakah* box for keeping your charity money.
- A list of phone numbers and e-mail addresses for friends from youth group and camp who are also going off to college. A handy form is included at the end of this book!

Hi, Rabbi, remember me? The kid who belched whenever he said *"baruch"*?

Before you close your boxes and load them into the car, make a few personal Jewish stops and calls. Go see your rabbi, youth group advisor, a favorite religious school teacher, or anyone who has been a part of your Jewish growth. Even if you didn't have a particularly close connection to anyone like that, find those you liked as a kid and seek them out for some Jewish advice. Tell them that you are off to college, and ask if they have any advice at all for you. You may be surprised at what they offer you. Remember, they knew you as a Jewish child and have watched you grow into a Jewish adult. They may have some insights that you haven't considered. Ask the same of your parents, grandparents, or other family members who have been influential in your personal Jewish growth. They may have some family advice, history, or wisdom that has served them well and could do the same for you. Don't be surprised if a dialogue is opened about dating Jews; we'll cover that issue in chapter 5. Remember that we are a people that has survived for over three thousand years, that we have wandered the world and adapted to it pretty successfully. You are not the first to move on with your life, and you won't be the last. Others may offer insights you will appreciate, so take advantage of them.

When Abraham was told by God to go and start the Jewish people, God told him, in chapter 12 of the Book of Genesis, *Lech l'cha,* "Go out. Leave

Three excellent and accessible Torah collections are *The Torah: A Modern Commentary,* edited by W. Gunther Plaut (New York: UAHC Press, 1981); *The Five Books of Moses,* by Everett Fox (New York: Schocken Books, 1997); and *Etz Hayim* (Philadelphia: JPS, 2001). A complete version of the *Tanach,* with both Hebrew and English text, is also published by the Jewish Publication Society.

Some wonderful books containing information on Shabbat rituals and songs are:
Frishman, Elyse C. *Birkon L'Shabbat: Blessings for the Table.* New York: CCAR Press, 1999.
Perelson, Ruth. *An Invitation to Shabbat.* New York: UAHC Press, 1997.
Shapiro, Mark Dov. *Gates of Shabbat: A Guide for Observing Shabbat.* New York: CCAR Press, 1996.
Stern, Chaim. *On the Doorposts of Your House.* New York: CCAR Press, 1994.
Teutsch, David, ed. *Shirim Uvrahot: Songs and Blessing.* Reconstructionist Press, 2000.

For an extensive anthology of Jewish music, look for *The Complete Shireinu: 350 Fully Notated Jewish Songs* (New York: Transcontinental Music, 2001), available from Transcontinental Music at www.transcontinentalmusic.com.

Still haven't made a decision on which college to attend? Kesher, the Reform Movement's college program, and Koach, the Conservative Movement's college program, both have good articles on-line that discuss Jewish criteria for choosing the campus that's right for you. You can find them at http://www.keshernet.com and http://www.koach.org, respectively. Both organizations run excellent e-zines as well. Koach's is available directly on its website and Kesher's is at http://www.myetone.org. Both are worth a look!

your home, your birthplace, and your parent's house so that I will bless you and make you great.'' Imagine that your parents, your family, your rabbi, your teachers, and your friends are all standing at the door of the home you grew up in, blessing you with the same words, *Lech l'cha*, ''Go and grow and create your own home and life, and make your name great.'' In leaving for college, you are about to embark on your adult life. Do well, study hard, be a mensch, and you too shall be a blessing to yourself, to all who have helped you come this far, and to the Jewish people.

Your Home away from Home

Most students come to college straight from their parents' house. Your room, your clothes, and your "stuff" have always been there to this point, and when you think of "home," that is the place that comes to your mind. For the majority of college students, starting college means leaving your parents' home and living on campus. Whether you live in a dorm, a fraternity or sorority house, an apartment, or house, chances are that entering your first year in college also means creating the first home of your own.

What exactly distinguishes this home from your parents' home? Many things, but they can all be summed up in one word: responsibility. At your parents' home, they were responsible for most or all of the daily expenses and obligations. Food, utilities, rent or mortgage payments, repairs, anything that cost money probably came out of their pocket. In college these expenses become your responsibility. Even if your parents are paying the cost of room and board for you in the dorm or giving you an allotment for rent and groceries, your living space is your responsibility. The lightbulb burns out; you have to buy a new one. You spill cherry Kool-Aid on the white carpet; you pay to have it cleaned. You need clean underwear; you wash it. You want a snack at 2:00 A.M.; you go to the store.

Responsibility for your home also means freedom to make it in your image. The walls can be covered in your choice of posters or wall-hangings. The fridge can be stocked with whatever you want to buy for it. The TV can be on whenever you want, and that underwear doesn't really have to be washed if you are into that sort of thing... It's your life and your space, your responsibility, and your decision.

The computer matched US up?!!

The tricky part though is that while your freshman home is your first home, it usually is not yours alone. Most campus dorms, apartments, and even Greek houses are usually shared space. This means that someone else, and often several other people, will be living with you in your room or suite of rooms. In fact, you may very well find yourself with less actual physical space in your first home than you had in your parents' home! Roommates are a fact of

2

Roommates, Microwaves, and Mezuzot:

Making Your First Campus Home a Jewish One

Learning to live in a dorm room, choosing your diet, sharing living space, and making it sacred for everyone

9

campus life, especially freshman year, and they can make or break your first experience in independent living.

The vast majority of incoming students are placed through the university's housing system. Colleges have a variety of systems for matching roommates, and they tend to take this process seriously because they know how tough it can be to manage with someone you can't live with. These systems usually break down into two categories. One category is a specific matching system, where schools get as much information as they can from every incoming student and then try to make as specific a roommate match as possible. This can include voluntarily grouping students in living units by ethnicity, academic major, cultural affiliation, or even gender for unique living experiences based on a common trait. The other category is general placement, where schools get basic information from each student, such as whether they smoke or mind music after a certain hour, and then match them up accordingly. This can result in roommates with, at least initially, little else in common other than that they both smoke and both like to stay up to watch late night TV.

While you may have little in common with your roommates at first, you may well find that you share a lot in common as you go through your first year of school together. If you have compatible personal habits such as how clean you like your living space or how much noise you can tolerate when you study, then you may find you can live together very well. Such seemingly small things should not be underestimated. Even if you wind up living with your best friend from high school, if you can't agree on how to best share or care for your living space, you can end up resenting each other's company and endangering the friendship. However, sharing personal space with someone from a similar cultural background can often help smooth the initial roommate edginess and provide a common background upon which to build not only a living relationship but a friendship as well.

To choose a Jew or not to choose a Jew— that is the question . . .

The first issue for a Jewish student in terms of roommates is, if given the choice, whether or not to request a Jewish roommate. Non-Jewish roommates can be excellent living partners and friends, and living with someone from a different background can give you a chance to learn about other life experiences and points of view. But on some campuses it is not uncommon to have a roommate who has never even met a Jew before. Choosing a

Jewish roommate certainly does not guarantee a smooth living relationship, but being Jewish might provide some good common ground upon which to build your roommate relationship. Jewish values, whether learned through a Jewish education or just from a loving Jewish family, are guideposts for life and human relationships. Someone who shares or at least understands your values has an immediate link with you before you ever meet. It also provides a cultural connection that can be expressed through common foods, a familiarity with Hebrew or Yiddish expressions, similar holiday and Shabbat experiences, and even a shared Jewish belief or understanding of God. Living with someone who understands without explanation why you have to skip school on Yom Kippur, why you might not eat pepperoni on your pizza, why you can't eat pizza at all during Passover, and why you feel compelled to help the helpless and repair the world can make a living relationship a lot less stressful over the course of that first year at school.

If you should choose or be placed with a non-Jewish roommate though, it is of course likely that you will be able to find shared interests, tastes, and values as well. Maybe you are both athletes, you are both premed, you both love the same music, or you are both vegetarians. If so, or even if you are both open to finding what you have in common and exploring your differences, you will be able to find a way to live together in relative harmony. But what can you do to create commonality and build bridges, in the case of either a Jewish or non-Jewish roommate, if you seem to be completely mismatched? First of all, remember that we are all *b'nei Adam,* children of Adam, fellow human beings. Religion and culture are important common ground, but we all have a common humanity that provides a basis for relating to each other if we just keep an open mind and try. In fact, one of the first and most central teachings in Jewish tradition is the idea that all humans are made *b'tzelem Elohim,* in the image of God. This idea commands us to see the humanity in even the messiest or most annoying of roommates. With some sincere effort, someone with seemingly little in common with you on move-in-day could end up being your closest friend by spring exams. Whether or not you end up with Jewish or non-Jewish roommates though, there are some basic issues you and your roommates should discuss before you arrive on campus.

Hi! You don't know me, but could I borrow your VCR?

The university housing office will usually send you the names and addresses of your future roommates in advance, so you should contact them as soon as

Jews keep a variety of levels of kashrut (kosher). Some maintain a strict separation of milk and meat products, avoid pork, shellfish, and other non-kosher foods, and limit consumption of prepared foods to only those that were prepared under rabbinical supervision. People who are that observant may choose not to eat at any restaurant that is not also under rabbinical supervision nor in any kitchen that is not strictly kosher. Other Jews keep only "biblical" kashrut, that is, not eating any food forbidden to us in the Torah and not eating meat and milk products together, but not limiting themselves to items or restaurants under rabbinical supervision. Still others keep only cultural vestiges of kashrut, like not eating pork just because their family has never eaten it, and still others follow no level of kashrut at all. Some Jews have started to keep what is being called eco-kashrut. According to this interpretation, since the word kashrut means "clean," we should eat only clean foods that do not harm the environment or us. For some that means strict vegetarianism, while others limit themselves to only organic foods.

you can. Try calling them because nothing can replace the sound of a real voice. If you are not sure what to say, look back over your college application essays and see what you told others about yourself. Jot down the positive things that jump out at you from them, and then add other things you would want people to know about you. Make a list of things you would like to know about others, both as a person and as a roommate. When you call, you can refer to these notes if you feel insecure or stuck in the conversation. You will be amazed how quickly the ice will be broken. Be sure to ask about items you would like to have in your living space for common use, like a refrigerator or TV, so that you know who will be bringing what.

Some of those items might actually spark a conversation about religion, especially items related to food. If you keep any level of kashrut, the Jewish dietary laws that are an important part of our tradition, then sharing joint cooking and food arrangements with roommates who do not can be of concern even if they are Jewish. If keeping kosher is not a priority for you, then food will not be an issue in your roommate relationship. However, if you come from a home that keeps kosher on any level, it will be helpful to discuss with your parents what they think is realistic for you to observe in a roommate situation. Remember, it is shared space, so compromise may be necessary. Your parents can help you determine your options, because when it comes to shared cooking and food supplies, you have to be clear for yourself what level of kashrut, if any, you want to keep. If this is an actual concern for you, don't be afraid to raise it with your roommates. Judaism customarily sees food and the process by which we prepare and eat it to be a holy act, and kashrut is a process of purity related to what we take into our bodies. Most other religions have purity rituals of their own, and when it is explained to your roommates that kashrut is one of ours, they will often understand and be willing to accommodate you. Such discussion can also help build links between you by learning about each other's personal lives and can help smooth out your living arrangements. Incidentally many, although not all, college food services can make arrangements for kosher food through the cafeteria, campus Hillel, or other source if it is requested in advance when you register for housing.

Once you have worked out who brings the TV and whether or not you will have ham in your refrigerator, the next issue is what will go on your walls. People like to personalize their space with pictures, art, posters, diplomas, or other things that remind them of the lives they left at home and the things they value the most. For many, that includes religious articles. It is not uncommon for Christians of various persuasions, Buddhists, or people of other faiths (although not Islam) to want to hang a cross, crucifix, or other religious icon on their wall as a reminder of their faith or even as a vehicle for observance. For Jews such icons are difficult to understand because we do not believe in a physical God or in any type of heavenly being in human form such as a saint. God for us is intangible, and having religious iconography on our walls can be uncomfortable, especially if we have ever experienced any religiously based anti-Semitism. We may have grown up with Jewish art on the walls, but it was not considered to be a picture of God.

The best way to tackle this question is to ask yourself before you contact your roommates, "Is there anything that would make me uncomfortable if it was hanging on the wall of my living space?" If the answer is yes, then ask yourself if there is any way or time you could accept having such things hanging somewhere specific. Perhaps you can accept them on the wall if your roommates need them for prayer and hung them up only then. Perhaps you would feel comfortable if they hung them over their beds or desks and not in a more common area. Perhaps they will not trouble you at all. The important thing is to be honest with yourself about this question and assess your comfort level. Then bring it up with your roommates. Ask them if they plan to hang any religious symbols in the room and, if so, what kind. If they are planning to do so, ask them to tell you about it and what it means to them. If you are still uncomfortable with the idea, explain why. Ask if there is a compromise that you can both live with, like those that you have already thought about in advance, or perhaps they can suggest some other idea. With goodwill and a little effort, you can reach a compromise that respects all of your needs.

Thanks, but no thanks . . . —just in case

Living with someone with a different belief system can be interesting and educational. There is, however, one thing to be aware of with a Christian roommate that you may not encounter until you are already living together. Though they are not the majority, some Christian denominations teach that only Christianity can provide you with an eternal afterlife. Many of these denominations also believe that it is incumbent upon their followers to evangelize to non-Christians in order to "save" their souls from damnation. It sometimes happens that Jewish students get inadvertently paired with students like this, and it can make your living arrangement difficult and uncomfortable. You have a right under almost any college's residence hall policy not to be "witnessed" to and certainly not to have to live in a situation

"Witness" is a Christian term for telling others about an individual's personal religious beliefs, experience, and connection to Jesus in hopes of persuading the listener to adopt a similar belief. For members of some Christian denominations, this is a religious obligation.

Two helpful resources for gaining a better understanding of other religions and their perspectives on various issues are Arthur J. Magida, ed., *How to Be a Perfect Stranger: Vol. 1* (Woodstock, Vt.: Jewish Lights Publishing, 1995) and Arthur J. Magida, ed., *How to Be a Perfect Stranger: Vol. 2* (Woodstock, Vt.: Jewish Lights Publishing, 1999). For help in dealing with missionaries, cults, or simply Christians who don't get why Jews don't believe in Jesus, see the materials put out by Jews for Judaism. You can find them on the web at www.jewsforjudaism.org.

where that is an issue. Try to persuade such roommates to respect your beliefs and not impose theirs upon you, but feel free to go to your residence hall director or the director of your college's residence life office and ask for a room transfer if the problem persists. If you cannot get any assistance from the university system, call the Hillel rabbi on campus, a Jewish faculty member, a local rabbi, or even your home rabbi and ask for help. This type of situation happens infrequently, but it can happen.

It could also happen that your roommate might not be a person who proselytizes but rather has preconceived notions about Jews that may initially shock or offend you, like an assumption that all Jews are wealthy or that Jews are responsible for the death of Jesus. Sometimes assumptions like these are pure anti-Semitism, but more often they are just the result of ignorance and can be corrected through honest dialogue. The key to a great roommate relationship is mutual respect and communication, and that will usually lead to a successful resolution of an unintentional offense. If that cannot be achieved in situations such as these, however, then do not be afraid to seek out help.

Hanging it up where you are hanging out

Finally, one last question to ask yourself before you call your roommates: do you want to put a mezuzah on your door at school? It is customary to hang one upon the doorposts of one's home, and chances are there is one on the front door of your parents' house. It does not make the home Jewish, but rather signifies that a Jew lives there. It is an ancient tradition to hang a mezuzah on the doorpost of the house when you move in to symbolize the commitment of the Jewish inhabitant to God and Judaism. Despite folk beliefs to the contrary, having a mezuzah on your doorpost does not provide any spiritual protection, nor is there any spiritual danger by not having one. But it is a commandment that can be found in the Torah to mark our homes in this way as a reminder of each Jew's relationship with God, and it has come to be an important symbol for Jews. If you decide that you would like to observe this custom at school, ask your roommates if they are comfortable with your hanging a mezuzah on your dorm room door. As they may not know what a mezuzah is, explain that it is the traditional sign of a Jewish home and that it is different than a crucifix or statue used for prayer. It can be comforting for you to see such a symbol when everything else on campus feels so far from home.

Many Jews today choose to honor the commandment through hanging a mezuzah only on the front door. But traditionally, mezuzot are hung on every doorframe in the house except for the bathroom. If you have a fence around your home, the gate frame would even have a mezuzah!

If your roommates are uncomfortable with your mezuzah, it is important that you ask them where their discomfort comes from and how you can help alleviate it. This is an understandable reaction, especially if you have expressed discomfort with one of their religious symbols. There may be a need for more dialogue between you about religion. They may just not be familiar enough with Jews and Judaism to understand exactly what you are talking about until they see it. Regardless of the reason, it is important that you communicate with and respect each other. If your roommates will not accept a mezuzah on your doorpost under any circumstances though, you have three choices. You can agree not to hang it up without their consent and bring it up at a later time if you become more comfortable and trusting of each other; you can express concern to the residence life office that you and your roommate may be incompatible and that you may want to change roommates later; or you can consult a rabbi for advice on how to handle the specific situation. Do not hang it up without your roommates' agreement though; it may become more uncomfortable for you with it than without it. In the vast majority of cases, it will be fine with your roommates for you to hang a mezuzah, and it would be a wonderful roommate relationship builder to invite them to participate in the hanging of it with you. Below is a description of how to hang a mezuzah either alone or with roommates. It's an easy and enjoyable mitzvah and a real sign of beginning your own independent adult life in your first home!

Hanging a mezuzah is easy and a great start to make your new place your home. Follow these instructions and you will have it up in no time!

1. If you did not bring a mezuzah from home, call your campus Hillel or local synagogue to ask how to acquire one. They can even be ordered on-line!

2. Decide where you are going to hang the mezuzah. Tradition teaches us to have one on every doorpost of our home, but many people in shared space just put one on the doorpost outside their own room. However many you choose, check the doorpost to see what material it is made of. The door frame is the part of the door that frames it when it is closed. The post is the part of the frame that you can see from the outside of the closed door that faces in toward the door. Determine if it is wood or metal.

These are the English translations of the Hebrew texts that are in the mezuzah: Deuteronomy 6:4–9 and 11:13–21.

Hear, O Israel! The Eternal God is our God, the Eternal God alone. You shall love the Eternal God your God with all your heart and with all your soul and with all your might. Take to heart these instructions with which I charge you this day. Impress them upon your children. Recite them when you stay at home and when you are away, when you lie down and when you get up. Bind them as a sign on your hand and let them serve as a symbol on your forehead; inscribe them on the doorposts of your house and on your gates. (Deuteronomy 6:4–9)

If, then, you obey the commandments that I enjoin upon you this day, loving the Eternal God your God and serving Him with all your heart and soul, I will grant the rain for your land in season, the early rain and the late. You shall gather in your new grain and wine and oil—I will also provide grass in the fields for your cattle—and thus you shall eat your fill. Take care not to be lured away to serve other gods and bow to them. For the Eternal God's anger will flare up against you, and He will shut up the skies so that there will be no rain and the ground will not yield its produce; and you will soon perish from the good land that the Eternal God is assigning to you.

Therefore impress these My words upon your very heart: bind them as a sign on your hand and let them serve as a symbol on your forehead, and teach them to your children—reciting them when you stay at home and when you are away, when you lie down and when you get up; and inscribe them on the doorposts of your house and on your gates—to the end that you and your children may endure, in the land that the Eternal God swore to your fathers to assign to them, as long as there is a heaven over the earth. (Deuteronomy 11:13–21)

3. Your mezuzah may come with small nails and holes for them on the assumption that your doorpost is made of wood, but if it is metal then get yourself some strong double-faced adhesive tape or Velcro and place a strip along the back of the mezuzah.

4. Stand outside the room with the door closed. The mezuzah will be attached to the inside surface of the doorpost that is on your right as you are facing the door, about a third of the way from the top. If you have a door that closes flush with the frame, it will be attached to the outside surface of the doorpost at the same height.

5. Before you attach the mezuzah, you and/or your roommates may want to read the following out loud or just say what it means to you to take this special step:

> This mezuzah is a symbol of a new home and a new life here at college, a life that will hopefully be one of learning, growth, challenges, and excitement. It is the first of many new homes, but it is among the most special because it is the first adult home and a symbol of new independence. May all who enter here know peace and contentment, joy and blessings.

6. Recite the following blessing before you affix the mezuzah:

Baruch atah Adonai,	בָּרוּךְ אַתָּה יי
Eloheinu melech haolam,	אֱלֹהֵינוּ מֶלֶךְ הָעוֹלָם,
asher kid'shanu b'mitzvotav	אֲשֶׁר קִדְּשָׁנוּ בְּמִצְוֹתָיו
v'tzivanu likboa m'zuzah.	וְצִוָּנוּ לִקְבּוֹעַ מְזוּזָה.

We praise You, Eternal God, Sovereign of the universe: You hallow us with Your mitzvot, and command us to affix the mezuzah.

7. Attach the mezuzah, being sure to affix it securely but temporarily so you can easily remove it when you move out the following year. *Mazal tov!*

Hello, Grandma?
Can you FedEx me one of your honey cakes please?

Around the time you settle into your new schedule on campus and begin to make the cultural transitions to college life, along come the High Holy Days: Rosh HaShanah, Yom Kippur, Sukkot, and Sh'mini Atzeret/Simchat Torah. For most North American Jews, the first two are the most important community holidays of the year. These four holidays fall over the course of a three-week period usually starting in mid to late September, and depending on whether your school is on a semester or quarter cycle, they usually fall at the beginning or middle of the autumn term. Depending on when they fall on the academic calendar, this can create some scheduling hassles for you.

The High Holy Days are, for most college students, the initial experience that defines your Judaism vis-à-vis that of your parents. Case in point: You probably observed the High Holy Days as your parents did when you lived in their home. When you lived at home, you probably missed school for at least the first day of Rosh HaShanah and for Yom Kippur in order to go to synagogue as a family. Unless you went to a high school with a large Jewish population that closed entirely on those days, your parents would have reminded you when to tell your teachers that you would be absent and arranged with the school for an excused absence so you could get your make-up work. If they observed two days of Rosh HaShanah, so did you. You attended services at the synagogue where they attended. If they stayed for a full day of services, perhaps you did as well. Even if you did do something different on those days, you most likely did it only with their permission. Perhaps the High Holy Days were good experiences for you. Or maybe you were one of many teenagers who did not have positive experiences on them. Either way, your High Holy Day experience was dependent on your parents' decisions. Now all of those decisions that your parents made for you about how you observed and experienced the High Holy Days are your decisions. You are an adult now, and you can and must decide for yourself how to observe the High Holy Days.

So how do you start to make these decisions? First take out your Jewish calendar and check it against your school calendar. When do the High Holy Days fall this year on the academic calendar?

Not Your Mother's Chicken Soup:

How to Handle Your First High Holy Days Away from Your Family

Choosing your own religious practice and assuming your own religious responsibilities

At some schools on the quarter system, during years when the High Holy Days fall early in the autumn, classes have not even started yet. These same schools often have problems during other years with one of the holidays falling during orientation week, so check closely. If you find such a conflict, first decide if you want to be at home with your family or on campus for orientation. This can be a difficult decision. While it may be familiar and comfortable to be with your family, the orientation experience is a key part of transitioning to campus life. Contact the campus Hillel, Jewish student advisor, or chaplain and ask what accommodations are being made for incoming Jewish students. Many schools on the quarter system arrange early move-in dates and alternative orientation activities for Jewish students. If your campus does not have a Hillel or other Jewish student advisor, which may be the case at a school with a small Jewish population, contact the directors of student and residence life or even a gentile college chaplain and explain the problem. They are usually willing to help arrange for students to get settled without forcing them to miss observing the holiday.

On the majority of North American campuses, though, the High Holy Days fall during the midst of the autumn academic term, often on a class day and not infrequently in conflict with a quiz or midterm. Unlike your local high school, where a note from your parents was usually sufficient to excuse your holiday absence, the college may or may not easily accommodate your missing classes and tests for religious reasons. There is no legal requirement that the school automatically accommodate your absence if it deems the request to be unreasonable. That means that as an adult it is your responsibility to arrange ahead of time for your absence with your instructors, and not afterwards. Most schools have clear policies about requiring accommodations from classroom instructors for religious absences about which they receive advance notice from the student, but universities tend to give broad latitude to the instructors about how they structure their class attendance requirements and make-up options for missed work and exams. The campus administration will not intervene if you are denied make-up work because you did not notify your instructor in advance. This is not an anti-Jewish issue but rather the reality of the diverse communities found on most college campuses. There are literally dozens of religions represented in the average student population, and students miss class for religious reasons all of the time. Without a fair expectation of responsibility from the students who rightfully choose to miss class to observe their religious practices, classroom instructors would be constantly dealing with make-up work and rescheduling exam times. An expectation of advance notice allows the instructor to plan accordingly if an absent student needs to make alternative arrangements. Two weeks' notice is a good suggested time frame in case there are any difficulties to be overcome in approving your absence.

Occasionally a student comes across an instructor who may not be knowledgeable about the importance of the High Holy Days in Judaism or who has tough attendance requirements and therefore asks for some proof regarding the validity of your absence. Here a note from your local Hillel or home rabbi will usually serve as the required proof. If you do encounter an instructor who is not willing to accommodate your advance request for a religious absence, do not hesitate to go to the chair of that academic department for help and intervention, or to your class dean, the college vice president for academic affairs, or the campus ombudsman. Of course consult the local Hillel staff or Jewish student advisor for help as well. In almost all cases, these situations can be resolved with little difficulty once the proper staff has been notified of the problem.

Hmmmm . . . *Kol Nidrei* or biochemistry?

All of this presupposes that you actually are choosing to observe the High Holy Days. But there are some students who do not feel comfortable missing class even for religious reasons. This can be a tough call—miss a lecture or even an exam, important parts of academic life, or miss services, an important part of Jewish religious and communal life. As you deal with making a choice, realize that this is part of your newfound adulthood. As an adult, no one can make you attend services anymore if you do not want to.

If you grew up resenting being dragged to services, it is understandable that you might not want to attend services now that you have a choice. Choosing to skip Rosh HaShanah or Yom Kippur is a move toward independence—making choices about what you want to do and not what your parents want for you. But if you are thinking about not observing the holidays as a way to declare your new freedom, think for a minute about your choice. Did you dislike the holidays as a kid? What really made the High Holy Days such a bad time for you? Was it because of family stress that surfaced then due to the visit of annoying relatives, or painful moments due to divorced or deceased parents? Did the services seem foreign or irrelevant? Were you uncomfortable because you could not follow them? Did you resent being taken away from other activities on those days?

Did you have a lousy religious school experience and being at services was just another reminder of that experience?

Because we live in a predominantly Christian country, we often see movies and television shows that feature various family conflicts centered around Christmas. Dysfunctional families trying to act appropriately for the twenty-four hours of Christmas or depressed and suicidal characters suffering through it alone are just two common plot lines. These are so prevalent each year because they are true; Christmas is not always a merry time for everyone because of personal and family reasons. The same is true for us around the High Holy Days. Because schools and businesses do not usually close for the Jewish holidays, there can be stress involved in getting the family together to celebrate. And when families do gather, they do not always get along. Add to that the fact that Rosh HaShanah and Yom Kippur are about examining errors of the past year, and it can be a pretty uncomfortable time before you even get to the synagogue. The services themselves can be foreign if you only go to synagogue twice a year for the High Holy Days. The Hebrew may seem like Greek to you, and what prayers you may have once learned may now be fuzzy at best. All of this can be frustrating and even embarrassing. Furthermore, the services can seem incredibly long in today's high-speed modem, sound-bite world, and all of this talk about sins and transgressions and who shall live and who shall die can feel oppressively heavy. With all that on the plate, who can blame you for choosing to go to class instead?

So here is a challenge: if you are a college student who is considering exercising your new adulthood by rejecting the High Holy Days, consider rejecting your uncomfortable childhood memories instead and try having an adult Jewish experience. Consider the basis on which you are making your decision. If the majority of your Jewish experience and education ended at or even before your bar or bat mitzvah, think about the fact that you were at most thirteen when you stopped any regular involvement with Jewish religious practice. That was at least five years ago, right? Can you think of anything else you make decisions about based on what you knew in elementary or middle school? You are in college now! You may be shocked how different things can be with some maturity and time under your belt. Take a look at the following suggestions before you make your choice whether or not to observe the High Holy Days:

- If you have the opportunity to go home for the holidays, think about what might be different there. Will there be friends and family whom you'll want to see? You are older and more grown up. What will other people whom you knew as a child look like now? How will they react to you now that you're older and more mature? It might actually be fun to find out. If you choose to stay at school, what will it really be like to be away from your family and friends during the holidays? Even if you hated services, what about those family dinners and break-fasts that you attended each year? Will it be lonely to be away from them?

- If you stay on campus, there will be other students on your campus missing their family and friends and the familiarity of the holidays. Consider attending at least some meals at Hillel or a local synagogue and making new friends with whom you share the common bonds and experiences of being Jewish. If by some chance there are no holiday meals offered on your campus, then consider getting together at someone's apartment or even at a restaurant with other Jewish students to mark the occasion together. You might be amazed by how much you have in common.

See chapter 4 on how to make your own Shabbat experience on campus and for tips on how to host a holiday meal!

- Think about attending at least some of the High Holy Day services at Hillel or wherever they are provided on campus. This is not your parent's synagogue. These services are made up of students from different places and backgrounds, and they may be much more interesting than what you are used to from home. Furthermore, being in a congregation of people who are almost all your own age is an entirely different experience than being in a congregation of families. The feeling is different, the energy is different, the fasting is different. Services for students generally allow opportunities for involvement and participation. High Holy Day services need not be seen as performance art, and student services can be quite empowering, reminding you in no uncertain terms that you are not a child anymore. Moreover, as an adult, you may come to experience those empowering differences as a real rejuvenation of your spiritual self. You may even come to appreciate the holidays in a way that you could not have as a child.

- Try to imagine what you as an adult can experience in services. Even if the Hebrew is foreign or uncomfortable, follow along with the English translation and read it with an adult eye. These services are written as a dialogue with God about old mistakes and new beginnings, eternal truth and human error, and making Jewish choices in a non-Jewish world. It is not necessary to read the prayers literally. Try reading them as poetry or metaphor. They are variations of prayers that Jews have been sharing with God for thousands of years. As a child, you could not have grasped

If you go to High Holy Day services, don't forget to take some of those personal prayer items listed in chapter 1 that you might have brought from home, like a *tallit* or prayer book. They might help you feel more at home in a new place of prayer.

It is also possible to organize and create your own High Holy Day services. See the "High Holiday Initiative Program Pack" put out by Kesher. It can be obtained by either e-mailing Kesher@uahc.org or calling 212–650–4070.

the enormity of these ideas, but as an adult you can begin to access them on an intimate level.

- If you attended religious school and now feel guilty or ignorant because you cannot remember much of it, or if you never had a Jewish education as a child, consider this: A lot of anxiety about the High Holy Days stems from the "twice a year" practice discussed earlier. Religious ritual is just that, a type of customary habit, and if it is not acquired and engaged in regularly, it can easily be forgotten. Did you do something in elementary school or junior high regularly that you no longer do now, like play an instrument or a sport? Can you do that as well today as you could then? Probably not if you have not done it in a while. When you practiced regularly for concerts or games, you became familiar with your instrument or position. Once you stopped practicing and playing though, your skills atrophied and you got rusty. The same is true for Jewish ritual. You may have practiced it more regularly in preparation for your bar or bat mitzvah, and your family may have celebrated Shabbat regularly in some way when you and your siblings were usually home on Friday nights for dinner and services with the family. But perhaps once the bat or bar mitzvah was over and you were old enough to get involved in football, cheerleading, band, or some other activity that pulled you away from home on Friday nights, you fell out of practice and got Jewishly rusty. Maybe it is time to consider acquiring or brushing up those Jewish skills a bit between this Rosh HaShanah and the next. Hillel, Judaic studies courses, and even the Internet can provide you with the help you need to make yourself ritually comfortable as an adult any day in services as well as on the High Holy Days. The Jewish confidence that comes with Jewish competence is worth the extra effort.

- Consider calling your parents and talking with them about what it is like to be away from home for the holidays. Ask for their advice as an adult. What did the holidays mean to them when they were your age? What do the holidays mean to them now? What do they hope the holidays mean to you now? As an adult, are you satisfied with their answers? In light of their answers, what do you want for yourself? Remember, their choices and your choices may be different now, and that is OK as long as your choices are sincere ones. As Jewish tradition teaches that the days prior to the High Holy Days should be used to seek forgiveness from others, you may want to clear the air over any lingering disagreements or uncomfortable issues while you have them on the telephone. A Jewishly responsible adult can honor his parents by making amends with them about past problems from childhood and use the new year to build a new adult relationship with them.

The High Holy Day season consists of more than just Rosh HaShanah and Yom Kippur. Sukkot comes right behind Yom Kippur, and Sh'mini Atzeret/Simchat Torah comes at the end of Sukkot week. Many Jews have come to think of these as children's holidays. Sukkot is an agricultural holiday where we are supposed to build booths in which to eat and sleep in the fields as our ancestors did during the harvest. Since most North American Jews are city dwellers or suburbanites, much of the meaning and observance of Sukkot has become obscured. Many Jews rely on their synagogue to build a community sukkah, and it ends up being used primarily by the religious school students. Similarly, Simchat Torah, the holiday that marks the renewal of the annual Torah reading cycle, is often thought of as a children's holiday because of its festive synagogue-based nature. Since children are often in the synagogue more regularly than many of their parents in today's busy world, the celebration of the holiday is often designed with them in mind. One of the joys of campus Judaism is that it is not by nature pediatric. Most people attending a Hillel event are between eighteen and twenty-five, and the holiday celebrations reflect a young adult constituency. Reexperiencing Sukkot as an adult through helping to build or decorate a campus sukkah, enjoying a meal with your peers in a sukkah, or being part of the festive hands-on experience of an adult Simchat Torah celebration is a great way to connect anew with the holidays you filed away as a part of your childhood. Check with your Hillel or Jewish contact on campus to see what's doing for these two great Festivals.

Jewish tradition teaches that God does not accept our prayers of forgiveness for our transgressions against God until we have sought to resolve our transgressions against each other. That is one of the reasons for the ten days between Rosh HaShanah and Yom Kippur. These ten days allow us to clear the air with each other before the big fast. This is not always easy to do, and not everyone forgives so easily either. The tradition teaches that you are required to ask someone for forgiveness up to three times, and if that person cannot find it in his or her heart to grant it, the transgression now lies with him or her and not with you. If a problem you have had with someone is weighing heavily on your conscience and you don't feel you know how to approach that person, seek guidance from a rabbi on how to go about making amends in difficult situations.

The first, second, seventh, and eighth days of Sukkot and Simchat Torah are Festival days and as such are treated religiously similar to Rosh HaShanah and Yom Kippur. Reform practice does not recognize the second and eighth days of Festivals for several reasons, which are outlined in the discussion about Passover. This means that only the first and last days of the Festivals are full holidays according to the standard calendar, though some Reform synagogues follow the traditional calendar. Jewish tradition discourages attending classes on the Festival days, but many Jewish students make a personal choice to attend classes on these days if they have already taken off for Rosh HaShanah and Yom Kippur. However, on many campuses the Festival events and celebrations tend to be shorter and geared around class schedules so you can participate in them easily and conveniently.

Shabbat—it's not just for b'nei mitzvah anymore

When you first get to campus and you want to connect with other Jews, there is no better place than a campus Shabbat dinner. Now that may seem a bit boring and not exactly your first choice for a Friday night, but consider how you may have experienced Shabbat in the past. Jewish tradition calls Shabbat God's gift to the world. Growing up, you may have experienced it as a gift of wonderful family and communal time, or you may have experienced it as an intrusion on your social life. Or maybe you never experienced it at all. Parents often want to instill knowledge of the customs and symbols of Shabbat in their children, so they light candles, make *Kiddush* over wine and *Motzi* over bread, and go to services fairly regularly on Friday nights or Saturday mornings. As children get older, events like soccer or drama or even academics often start to compete with religious school, and holiday observance can feel like a chore. The joy of Shabbat often gets lost along the way, and Shabbat comes to be perceived as an intrusion into the weekend rather than the highlight of the week. Even if you had many wonderful Shabbat experiences at a Jewish camp or youth movement event, in many cases these were created for you and you did not have to take a primary leadership role in ensuring that Shabbat was celebrated.

When people postpone any serious connection with Shabbat until they have children of their own, then the only memories that they have to share with their children are those of their own childhoods. But Shabbat has the potential to add so much to life. In a world of work with little time for rest and relaxation, Shabbat is an opportunity to enjoy the rest that God set aside for us and to indulge in the enjoyment of a regularly scheduled day off. Nowhere is this truer or more needed than on campus, where class schedules occupy your day and preparing for classes and finals occupies most of your nights and weekends. What free time you do have in between your academic work is often taken up by formalized socializing such as campus-wide events, fraternities and sororities, sports and other campus interests, or maybe even a part-time job. Despite all of the newfound independence, college students seem to get little time for themselves. Shabbat can give you that personal time.

4

Tailgates and Torah: Melding the Happiest Night on Campus with the Holiest Night of the Week

Merging your campus and Jewish life, unpacking your "Hebrew school baggage," and connecting with Shabbat

Shabbat is traditionally understood to be a full day, from sundown on Friday to sundown on Saturday, during which Jews are supposed to do no manner of work. It is a day to rest and reconnect with our families and ourselves, the Jewish community, and of course God. In reality, many Jews in North America tend to condense Shabbat into about four hours. When you were living at home, Shabbat might have involved a dinner at home with candles and *Kiddush* and a service at the synagogue. If a football game, concert, dance, or date happened to fall on Friday night or Saturday, you might have chosen to forgo the observance of Shabbat altogether. This conflict of American life is partially a conflict of modernity versus tradition. The custom of observing a full day of Shabbat was developed at a time when Jews lived together and were not an integrated part of the larger society. The entire community was Jewish and based itself on a Jewish calendar, so there were no other distractions from Shabbat. It was the one day off from a six-day workweek, and it was a time for rest and observance with your family and friends. When our ancestors came to America though, we were allowed to join and participate in a larger society. Suddenly we had options on Friday night and Saturday that we never had before, so we had to wrestle with the idea of Shabbat observance. The four major American Jewish denominations differ on the details of correct Shabbat observance, but all agree on the value of Shabbat.

Unlike synagogues, where each community sets its own standards of observances and celebrations, campus Jewish communities have to take into account the wide variety of Jews who study there. For the common good of everyone, they have to create communities that respect and support ideological differences. This community building is usually done through a Hillel or Jewish student union. And nowhere is this effort to find common ground more obvious than on Shabbat.

Hillels face two challenges with Shabbat. First, everyone comes from a different Jewish place. Some people are traditional and some are liberal. Some are observant and some are not. Some like to pray in one style and some in another and usually others in a third. Some may find that music enhances the prayer experience while others find music incompatible with their understanding of the laws of Shabbat. Egalitarianism can also be an issue, or even the time that services are scheduled to start. These differences have to be accommodated so that everyone finds some level of comfort in order to create a Shabbat community. Second, many students assume an erroneous stereotype about Shabbat from their childhoods or about Hillel in general and feel that their own Jewish identity will be challenged or threatened if they participate. These assumptions are often a result of negative childhood experiences (often referred to as "Hebrew school baggage"). These assumptions get further entrenched when someone sees him- or herself Jewishly through a child's eyes and avoids the development of an adult Jewish identity. The following are some thoughts about connecting to Shabbat on campus:

- With all of the changes in your world since you first came to campus and even from term to term, it can be nice to have a touchstone of stability in your week. A regular Shabbat experience with familiar foods and customs can serve as such a touchstone, and after spending all week in classes with people from diverse backgrounds, the connection with folks whose manner, language, beliefs, and experiences are similar to your own can be a real welcome experience. Besides, Shabbat dinners on campuses are usually free or entail only a small fee and can be a welcome break from cafeteria food!

- You are no longer a child preparing for a bar or bat mitzvah. Attending services is not about meeting someone else's expectations, but rather about time you spend focusing on your relationship with God. If you are not sure about whether or not there is a God, you can use the time to focus on your relationship with yourself. Also, there is often more than one Shabbat option on campus. Remember that campus Jews are a diverse group with different beliefs and practices sharing the same facilities. Feel free to hop around and try something new. You might be surprised and find a new style of worship that is more meaningful for you. If there is only one option and you don't like it, get involved and try to make it more to your liking. There are few set customs in campus Shabbat prayer groups— generally the tunes and styles change every year. Embrace the Jewish diversity and learn or teach something new! Feel free to make suggestions; you may make a real difference for yourself and others!

- Try hosting your own Shabbat dinner. If your parents always took care of such things at home this may seem foreign to you, but there is no reason you cannot host a great Shabbat dinner yourself. You don't need to make a fancy dinner unless you want to. Just a bunch of friends gathered at a comfortable place like someone's apartment (or even a dorm room) for a dinner that is a little better than ordinary makes for a great Shabbat. If you like to cook, great! If cooking means takeout, then make it good takeout. How about a potluck Shabbat dinner? It's about the people you are with, the time you spend together, and the atmosphere you create much more than the food. Good wine, good food, some candles and bread, a few blessings and you have the makings for a great campus Shabbat dinner that you can do yourself on your budget at your place regardless of what flavor of Judaism you embrace. All the basic blessings you'll need can be found in the appendix of this book. The blessings for Havdalah, at the close of Shabbat, are provided as well.

- Don't feel obligated to do what every one else seems to be doing at a Shabbat dinner. Many students reconnect to Shabbat when they come to campus and need time to refresh themselves with the basic customs and practices, or even to learn them. Campus life exposes everyone to new and different customs. This often includes an awareness that the various Jewish denominations observe or interpret the same customs and rituals differently. Furthermore, if you did not grow up observing Shabbat, the rituals may seem intimidating. Don't think you are inept or a "bad" Jew if things are unfamiliar. Rather, ask other students or Hillel staff to explain the rituals to you and to help you try them. If you are uncomfortable, feel free to leave and come back again to try another time. Don't stay if you don't want to be there, because that kind of discomfort is antithetical to the restful spirit of Shabbat. And you don't have to embrace every custom you see just to fit in. Judaism is at its best when Jews are forging their own connections through rituals and practices that mean something to them, and many customs and rituals have more than one interpretation. Ask about what customs mean and where they come from. Feel free to challenge them if you don't understand or agree with them. You will find rituals more meaningful if you believe in what you are saying or doing rather than just doing what others have said you are supposed to do.

- You came to college to gain knowledge that will allow you to survive and thrive in life, and you can gain Jewish knowledge there as well. Don't settle with what you do not know. If you never learned Hebrew as a child or did not pay attention to what was taught to you in religious school, don't use that as an excuse for not knowing anything as an adult. You will be amazed at the wisdom you can gain from our history and ethical values, and you have the ability to acquire the tools to do so. Shabbat can be the first step in acquiring and embracing your own adult Jewish identity.

To learn more about Shabbat, check out the Shabbat page of Clickonjudaism.org. The following are some good books on Shabbat:

Elkins, Dov Peretz. *A Shabbat Reader: Universe of Cosmic Joy.* New York: UAHC Press, 1998.

Isaacs, Ronald H. *Every Person's Guide to Shabbat.* Northvale, N.J.: Jason Aronson, 1998.

Perelson, Ruth. *An Invitation to Shabbat.* New York: UAHC Press, 1997.

Shapiro, Mark Dov. *Gates of Shabbat: A Guide for Observing Shabbat.* New York: CCAR Press, 1996.

Washofsky, Mark. *Jewish Living: A Guide to Contemporary Reform Practice.* New York: UAHC Press, 2001.

Wolfson, Ron. *Shabbat: The Family Guide to Preparing for and Welcoming the Sabbath.* 2nd ed. The Art of Jewish Living Series. Woodstock, Vt.: Jewish Lights Publishing, 2002.

To Greek or not to Greek—that is the question . . .

The primary reason any of us goes to college is to get a useful and meaningful education to ensure our economic and personal prospects for the future. However, none of us plan on spending our entire undergraduate lives in the library. Also on the list of reasons to go to college is to have a good time. Everyone defines having a good time differently, but for almost all of us it definitely involves other people. After all, a social life by its very definition requires other people with whom to socialize. You will make friends from all different parts of your campus life—dorm, class, activities, parties, the laundromat—just about anywhere you go on campus will be filled with the potential of making new friends. And chances are that at some point in your undergraduate career you will be encouraged to check out Greek life.

On many campuses, but certainly not all, Greek is chic. What is Greek? It is shorthand for the fraternity/sorority system, which consists of private, same-sex social organizations that students can join, based on certain shared ethics and ideals. These social organizations were at one time based on the philosophical thought of ancient Greece, and they adopted Greek letters to identify themselves, thereby becoming known as "Greek" houses. Students affiliate with these organizations in order to expand and enhance their social, experiential, and housing opportunities. Especially on large campuses, the Greek system can provide a way to meet and bond with people around a common institution and social schedule. Many universities permit their Greeks to own chapter houses for members to live in off campus, or suites or floors of dorms on campus, and they empower the houses to govern themselves appropriately in order to remain on campus.

The Greek system was originally developed as a campus social order at a time when it was normative for people to join clubs or fraternal organizations throughout the broader society. Until the twentieth century, fraternities and sororities were generally restrictive in their membership. Jews were not admitted to many Greek houses during that time, and so they founded their own houses. Today the Greek system is not officially restrictive, but it is still self-selecting. While most houses do not claim to prefer one particular ethnic or religious group over others, historical biases still influence who joins which houses. The mutual process of selection, usually known

Jews and Greeks: Making Friends from a Jewish Perspective

Deciding on fraternity/sorority life, finding a social rhythm, embracing diversity, pondering personal particularity, contemplating Hillel, and dating

If you are going to a school that does not have fraternities or sororities, or if you are just not interested in reading about them at this point, skip on ahead in this chapter to the section entitled "Jews: The World's Largest Fraternity!"

as "rush," allows for an informal selection of candidates through a mechanism usually known as extending "bids" based on compatibility with the current membership. Naturally the current membership often chooses "pledges" who are similar to themselves so that they will fit into their perception of the organization. So, while today there are few officially Jewish Greek houses left, Jews will still often join certain houses because there are many Jewish members.

There are three questions to ask when it comes to Greek life. One, should I join a Greek house? Two, as a Jew should I join a Greek house? Three, should I choose a Greek house that has been historically Jewish? Greek life can be incredibly fulfilling for many people, but it is not for everyone. Many people enjoy the sense of belonging and affiliation, and they enjoy the active social schedule that Greek life provides. Others prefer a more independent social life. Rush is designed as much to help participants decide if they should join any house at all as it is to help them decide which house.

If you choose to go Greek though, you need to keep in mind that for Jews, Greek life could be problematic. Greek life is designed to be encompassing of daily life. A Greek organization provides you with your social life, your friendships, your home and meals, and your ideals for daily living based on both the house's formal creed and informal customs. In short, it can give you the basics for daily living. However, these organizational basics could potentially conflict with Judaism. There are Greek organizations whose rituals and customs are based on Christianity or a philosophical ideal that might conflict with Judaism. It would not be uncommon for a member to be required to perform a ritual act that violates Jewish teachings, such as taking a membership oath on a Christian Bible. Many Greek houses serve foods from their kitchens that you may not feel comfortable eating. Even if you don't keep kosher, a lunch of ham and cheese sandwiches with a glass of milk just may not be something you are accustomed to eating. The favorite night to throw parties is often Friday night, and many houses require attendance at their social events as a condition of membership. Another required event, fall rush, could potentially conflict with the High Holy Days. As you define your own Jewish identity and practices, they may wind up conflicting with Greek life. There are many benefits to being Greek, but be aware that there could be possible conflicts as well.

The next question then, if you choose to go Greek, is should you join a historically Jewish Greek house? Until relatively recently, you would not have had the choice. Jews fought very hard on campuses during the last century to desegregate many discriminatory institutions in this country because we, like people of color, were often victims of that discrimination. This included campus Greek systems, and our parents and grandparents fought on many campuses for the opportunity to join any house they chose. On today's campuses, diversity is an important concept, and many campuses go to great lengths to celebrate, support, and nurture the wide variety of religious, ethnic, racial, and cultural groups represented in student bodies by establishing rules that place no barriers to access and success in any campus institution on those bases. As a result, few officially Jewish Greek houses exist anymore, although some are still Jewish in their ideological makeup. We have welcomed non-Jews, as we have demanded to be welcomed in their chapters.

Today very few historically Jewish houses are set up to accommodate religious practice as a house because they are now fully part of the Greek system and they want to fit in with the other houses in the system. Hence, there are few that have kosher kitchens or don't plan Friday night social events. While it is generally Hillel or another Jewish student organization that is seen as the place to go to connect with Judaism rather than the fraternities and sororities, a historically Jewish house does offer a better opportunity to accommodate your personal religious life, however you choose to express it. For example, you probably will not have to take that membership oath on a Christian Bible or swear a vow through Jesus. While the kitchen may not be kosher, those who want to keep some level of kashrut will probably find an accommodating attitude from the house, and the chef may not serve any overtly unkosher items anyway. You won't be penalized for coming late to a social event on Friday nights if you choose to go to services or Shabbat dinner, and there will probably never be a schedule conflict between rush and Rosh HaShanah. Most importantly, there will be others in the house who understand your culture and customs, the things that go beyond religion into the realm of ethnicity. Sunday bagels, matzah during Passover, a communal menorah at Chanukah, *bubbes,* going to a family bar mitzvah, sitting shivah— all of these and more will serve to increase your bonds together as brothers, sisters, and friends. This in no way, shape, or form takes away from an appreciation of diversity. Encouraging and promoting diversity is the just thing to do, and in addition it also ensures our rights and liberties as a group. Nothing should stop you from joining a predominantly non-Jewish house if you feel comfortable there, but you should be aware of the social and cultural distinctions that you may encounter in such a close-knit environment.

These national fraternities and sororities still formally maintain a distinctly Jewish emphasis: Fraternities: Alpha Epsilon Pi, http://www.aepi.org; Sigma Alpha Mu, http://www.sam.org; Zeta Beta Tau, http://www.zbt.org. Sororities: Alpha Epsilon Phi, http://www.aephi.org; Sigma Delta Tau, http://www.sigmadeltatau.org.

Jews: The world's largest fraternity

Whether you join a Greek house or not, you are probably going to encounter more diversity at college than you did growing up. Even if you went to a diverse high school, you still went home to a family that was pretty much the same as you. In addition, you may have had a Jewish social group outside of school. Now that you are in college, your roommates, floor mates, classmates, coworkers, and colleagues will probably be different from you in many ways. While that is exciting, challenging, and even fun, you may find yourself missing a common Jewish link with others. Joining a historically Jewish Greek house can go a long way toward making those links, but it is no guarantee. Furthermore, if you choose not to go Greek, you will still have the same concerns. Is it possible to foster a comfortable adult Jewish identity without feeling that it distances you from others? It is not discriminatory or exclusionary in any fashion to seek out others like yourself; rather, discrimination is based on keeping others away. As a Jew, you come from a uniquely diverse ethnic, cultural, and religious heritage, and it is built upon the idea of community. It is very hard to be Jewishly connected by yourself, and so it is natural to want to connect with other Jews. Hillel is the most common way to do that on college campuses.

Hillels are the center for Jewish life on most campuses; Jewish student unions or clubs serve that purpose on campuses without Hillels. These organizations provide social and cultural events that can be among the best on campus. They often sponsor intellectually or culturally exciting speakers and programs for the benefit of the entire campus. They coordinate social justice opportunities for the student body at large as well as for Jewish students. Most importantly, Hillels and other Jewish student organizations provide a gathering place for Jewish students seeking to connect with other Jews. They do so without judgment, expectation, or assumption of anyone's Jewish beliefs and practices, and they strive to be a welcoming place on a sometimes unwelcoming campus. It is very common for the Hillel staff to reach out when you arrive on campus to welcome and connect with you; consider that contact an open invitation. No one from Hillel will pressure you, but you will be welcome if and when you are ready to meet other Jews. Better yet, stop by the Hillel when you first come to campus and check them out.

Don't wait until the High Holy Days or Passover to try out your Hillel. Those are the busiest, craziest times for the Hillel staff as they frantically try to make sure that every Jewish student has the meals and services he or she

If you want to check out your Hillel before you even get to campus, try the www.hillel.org website, which has links to all of the campus Hillel web pages!

32

wants in order to celebrate the holidays. They will not have the time they would want to spend getting to know you and connecting you to the campus Jewish community. Furthermore, letting the holidays be your first exposure to Hillel will prevent you from seeing the wide variety of other things going on there during the rest of the year.

It's understandable if you don't automatically seek out your campus Hillel or Jewish student group. Hillels have historically had to wrestle with the stereotype that their organization was only for the socially inept or religiously observant. In addition, it can feel awkward to single yourself out as a Jew, even with other Jews. Maybe you assume it will be like religious school or youth group all over again, and you do not want to repeat that experience. Fortunately, today's Hillels are rarely like what they are stereotyped to be. Religious observance is but one factor of a Hillel's calendar, and many of them today are more like Jewish community centers for students than like synagogues. Hillels are designed to let you integrate your Jewish identity with your campus experience, and you will miss a great Jewish growth opportunity if you do not even give it a try. If, by the way, you should experience a less-than-open environment at your Hillel, talk immediately with your Hillel's director, and let him or her know. An important part of the job is helping you feel at home there. Also, don't hesitate to call your home rabbi and ask him or her to help express your feelings to the Hillel staff if you are uncomfortable doing it.

Challah or Communion wafers: Guess who's coming to dinner?

The issue of choosing Jewish versus non-Jewish roommates and Greek houses has already been addressed, so it's time to talk about dating. This isn't a discussion about sex—that's in chapter 8. "Dating" is defined in *Webster's New World Dictionary* as "a social engagement with a person of the opposite sex." On today's campus, the assumption of "opposite sex" is not always relevant, but the idea of "a social engagement" still holds true. Contrary to images from Hollywood, college students still spend a lot more time talking over coffee, attending a lecture or game, or catching a film than they do in bed. This is one of the great side benefits of college: there is so much on and around campus to see and talk about, and so many interesting people to see and talk with! High school dating was limited by where you could go as someone under eighteen, what curfew your parents set, and how much homework you had. In college you are master of your domain—your

> The Reform and Conservative Movements both have national college programs, called Kesher and Koach respectively, which offer wonderful web resources, conferences, and other opportunities. You can contact the college program of your religious movement for guidance and support. Check them out at http://www.keshernet.net and http://www.uscj.org/koach. The Orthodox community is served by Kedma at http://www.kedma.org. Additionally, it is important to point out that Reform, Conservative, Reconstructionist, and Orthodox Judaism are all very different on campuses than they are in synagogues. For explanations of each from the perspective of campus rabbis from each denomination, see the appendix.

schedule, your interests, your choices. In high school, you were usually limited to dating the same people you went to school with every day, but in college you meet people in class, in the dorm, at parties, at clubs, the library, at work, through mutual friends—the list goes on. Your group of friends will be much more diverse in college than in high school, and your dating choices and opportunities will be as well.

The question may then arise from parents, grandparents, friends, or even siblings: Are you dating Jews? Whom you date is your own business, isn't it? After all, diversity and individual freedoms are cornerstones not only of Western culture but of campus culture as well.

In case you're wondering why everyone is so concerned about this it may be helpful to have some perspective. At one time in Jewish history, Jews dating non-Jews just wasn't done. Dating was seen as a first step to marriage, and marriage between a Jew and non-Jew was a rare and frowned-upon event. This was a result of both religious prohibition as well as societal pressure and the urge for self-preservation. At times, there were also legal restrictions historically against Jews marrying non-Jews. In the second half of the twentieth century though, many people became fed up with social rules and restrictions. There had been two world wars and the Holocaust, events that were seen as being caused in part by legal bigotry and social separation, and people became disenchanted with such forms of authority and structure. The old social and religious boundaries were reevaluated, and people chose who they loved based on factors besides their skin color or ethnicity or faith. This was also a time of the creation of a new social order that celebrated the wants of the individual rather than the needs of the collective. As a result, interdating and intermarriage, which had been highly controversial during your grandparents' youth, became so common that by 1990 over half of the Jewish married community was intermarried. You may very well come from an intermarried family yourself. While all these events changed the face of marriage in North America, they also changed the face of Judaism worldwide.

Chances are, your college social life is not focused on finding someone to marry. Yet, you never know. Simply put, one thing leads to another. No matter what your social interest is at the moment, one day a date will lead to love, and love will lead to commitment, and commitment may eventually lead to marriage. Traditionally, Jewish parents had the duty and authority to find spouses for their children. Only in the last few hundred years (a drop in the bucket of Jewish time) have the children been free to find their own spouses. While parents have given up the formal role of choosing a spouse for their children, they still exercise informal influence by taking an active interest in whom their children are dating. They may express a concern for the preservation of Jewish traditions, customs, beliefs, and culture. Even families that are not concerned about the prospect of intermarriage may have these concerns. Some family members or friends may be more vocal and/or critical than others with you about this issue if they disapprove of your dating choices. Others could express their opinions in a way that is meant to make you feel guilty or to pressure you to see the issue their way, and you may even find yourself resentful of Judaism because of the pressure put upon you by some well-meaning relatives. With all of that in mind, dating can take on a whole separate dimension for Jewish students—it can sometimes feel like it's not just the two of you at the table, but your whole family and the entire Jewish community. So much for quiet conversation!

With all of this to consider, here are some suggestions regarding dating:

- Know what you want for your future. If you think that you will want to settle down and raise a family with a Jewish partner, you should try to make it a habit to date Jews. Even a casual date can unexpectedly lead to something serious—that's what makes dating fun after all—so it's a lot easier to think about this in advance rather than in the heat of the moment.

- If you choose to date others besides Jews—and there are of course lots of wonderful and exciting people in this world who are not Jewish—feel secure in whom you are as a Jew. Many interfaith couples hit major and painful roadblocks because the Jewish partner did not deal with his or her own Jewish identity and desires before the relationship got serious. Having the first conversation about religion when you've been invited to the family Easter dinner or when your mom wants to invite your new friend to the seder is *not* the best timing. Knowing your own beliefs and feelings about Judaism up front, both religiously and culturally, can help you know when and if the person you are dating has the same common core values and mutual respect for faith issues that you do. Love is a wonderful place to start a long-term relationship, but it is not always enough to keep it going without real common ground between the two parties.

- Be aware of the reality that many interfaith marriages have an extra hurdle to get over if either party values his or her own religious traditions and culture. Holiday observances, family expectations, and the education of children can all be contentious issues when the two people involved have

For an interesting look at how Jews in our generation are trying to connect with each other, look at two websites: http://www.jdate.com and http://www.frumster.com.

For more information on the issues with which interfaith families wrestle and possible solutions for them, check out the Outreach Department of the UAHC at http://uahc.org/outreach or the Jewish Outreach Institute at http://www.joi.org.

Different branches of Judaism view the conversion process differently. For a helpful list of questions and answers regarding conversion, go to http://uahc.org/outreach/becom.shtml. A good website that goes over all the options is the Conversion to Judaism Resource Center at http://www.convert.org.

different hopes or assumptions. Marriages have many points of negotiation in any case, and these areas of belief and practice will be that much more to deal with if you marry someone from another religion.

- Having children is probably even further from your mind than marriage. However, if you get seriously involved with someone of a different religion, it may be helpful to know some facts. Even couples from the same religion argue about their religious identity and practices and how best to raise their children. Much research has shown that raising children with two religions in order to give them the choice of faiths leads to great confusion. It takes a lot of effort and work by both parents to teach children enough about two religions over the course of their childhoods to enable them to make a comfortable and reasoned adult religious decision. That is in addition to the complicated emotional issue of having to choose one parent's religion over the other's. The majority of children who are raised to choose their religion as adults wind up choosing nothing. At the same time, raising children with no religion gives them no ethical grounding with which to compare and contrast religious ideals, no holidays or rituals to enrich the passage of time or mark milestones, and no sense of being part of a bigger community.

- If you choose to date non-Jews and find yourself in love and thinking life commitment, don't forget that asking your love to share your religion is not a bad thing to do. Many non-Jewish spouses throughout history have found warmth, acceptance, and meaning in Judaism and within the Jewish people, and if it means a lot to you, it can to them as well.

No pressure, but next week's exam is 100% of your grade...

Before you know it, the autumn term is coming to a close and exams are just around the corner. At some point around mid-November, you will realize with probably a bit of queasiness that these final exams are a large part or even all of your grade for the term. This is the flip side of all of that new freedom you have been enjoying—responsibility. You have only one or two chances to show you learned anything that entire term.

Jewish tradition understands learning to be a very different process than that modeled in most universities. Jews have historically engaged in learning through dialogue with teachers and study partners who are constantly assessing your knowledge base while you study and debate topics from the Torah, Talmud, and other Jewish sources. This model is called *chevruta*—"partner" learning. We literally debate our way through our texts and traditionally do so very loudly and proudly. The idea of sitting through lectures, only to be assessed at the end of the term through written exams, is contrary to the Jewish model of education, but it is the reality of the Western university system.

Final examinations are given on the assumption that you have been attending class regularly, taking careful notes during the lectures or keeping careful records of your lab work, and doing the required studying outside the classroom. They are usually given in one of three forms: a written, timed test in class (although computer versions of this are becoming more common), a graded research paper, or a series of in-class essays on covered topics. If you are carrying six or so classes your first term like first-year students at some schools, preparing for these exams can be incredibly daunting. There are different ways to prepare for exams, and students have to find the method that works best for their own style. However, there are some basic universal tips that can get you started.

- At the end of each week beginning with the first week of classes, take your class notes and edit them into a course outline. Reference your assigned textbook sections in the outline too. This will allow you to clear up your class notes and reinforce what you learned by editing and rewriting. By the end of the term, you will have a great study outline for exams.

6

December's Dilemmas and January in Jerusalem: Reality Check

Preparing for exams like a Maccabee, taking a look at the new you, reconnecting with family and friends at home, and connecting with new ones in Israel

- If you miss class for any reason, get the notes from someone else before the next class. That way you can be caught up so you do not waste another class sitting there and not understanding the lesson because you do not have the necessary information from the last class.

- Take advantage of the faculty office hours. These are set times each week when the faculty are in their offices to take questions from students. A few minutes of individual interaction with a professor can often be more productive than a full hour of lecture.

- Keep up with your required class reading assignments. Not only will the professor assume you know the material, but faculty sometimes call on students to answer specific questions to see if they are doing the reading.

- Get into the habit of writing a précis on books and articles you read for class. This will help you review and will allow you to access what you have read and learned from that reading long afterwards.

- Take study breaks. As hard as studying can be, you need to balance it with relaxation. Go to the movies, work out, jog, e-mail friends, go to Shabbat dinner, do whatever you enjoy that allows you to decompress. At the same time though, study first and then relax; it is always easier to take a break than to get started!

- Even if you know that the exam will be a research project, preparing for the class as if you had to take an exam will benefit you immensely. You will have a good compiled resource on the course for future use, and it will help you narrow your choice of research topics.

I could use a good miracle right around now!

Chanukah often falls in the midst of final examinations. It provides you with a great study break opportunity if you set aside a few minutes each night to light the *chanukiyah*. If you did not bring one from home, your Hillel may be able to provide you with one. They may also sponsor a lighting of their own each night of the holiday. If your dormitory has a restriction on lighting candles for fire code reasons, don't be afraid to approach the hall director for an exemption or to propose a compromise like lighting one for the entire hall in a public space where it can be watched by dorm staff. Ask your Hillel staff or local rabbi for help with this negotiation if you feel uncomfortable proposing it yourself. Also, a Chanukah party is a great study break or end of term event. All you have to do is invite a group of friends over, buy the latke ingredients (premade boxed mixes are good too), provide some good music and your favorite beverages, and you are all set! If you live in a dormitory,

Chanukah is the eight-day winter holiday that celebrates the defeat of the oppressive Syrio-Greeks by Jewish guerrilla forces in ancient Israel during the second century B.C.E.

reserve a kitchen space for the cooking and a lounge space for the party itself. Either way, have everyone help with the potato shredding and onion peeling, and fry up a great time.

The Chanukah story is an apt metaphor for college life. In the second century B.C.E. in ancient Israel, the Greeks were in control. Their policy was to "hellenize" the areas under their control, which meant to change the social and cultural structure of the community to reflect Greek ideals, which they saw as more advanced than other cultures. This split the Jews in ancient Israel into two camps: the zealots, who wanted to resist the Greek culture being offered to them and remain traditionally Jewish; and the Hellenists, who wanted to accept and incorporate Greek culture into Jewish life. These two groups fought each other as to which group would control the Temple. The Greeks mistook this violent dispute as a rebellion, and they suppressed all Jewish practice, which then caused the revolt led by the Maccabees, originally part of the zealots. Because these two different approaches to Judaism could not cooperate, all of Judaism was almost lost. It is a good lesson to remember on campus.

Throughout Jewish history, Jews have fought over defining what it means to be Jewish, and this challenge is with us even today. On a college campus, such a judgmental approach to this challenge is divisive and dangerous. College is a time of intellectual challenge and exploration, learning mutual respect in the face of differences of opinion, and celebrating diversity while embracing particularity. Campus Jewish communities that judge and pigeonhole each other run the risk of imploding—and repeating the mistake of the Jews of the second century B.C.E. College is the best time to develop and explore your Judaism and to experiment with what you truly think and believe. Hillel's function is what is thought of today as "cross-denominationalism." This means that Hillel does not identify or support any one denomination over the other, but rather works with all of them and offers as many choices as possible to the students. Hillels often run multiple services for Shabbat and holidays, sponsor activities across the religious spectrum, set up Jewish learning experiences from all denominational angles, and equally support student religious life and choices. Students today have the opportunity to explore and sample Jewish thought and practices different than the ones in which they were raised, and they often are in a state of flux from year to year as they search for their own Jewish path. Here are a few things to consider as you begin to think about your personal definition of Judaism:

Patti Aaron, the author's mom, has always made the best latkes. The author used this easy recipe for years at his campus Chanukah parties! This recipe will make around eighteen latkes—feel free to experiment with amounts and proportions if you want more or less. You'll need 12 regular potatoes, 4 baseball-sized onions, 2 eggs, salt and pepper to taste, $1/4$ cup flour, $1/2$ cup corn oil, frying pan, food processor with grater disk or hand graters, paper towel, mixing bowl and spoon, serving pan and spatula, and sour cream and/or applesauce and/or cinnamon and brown sugar.

1. Preheat pan with oil in it on the stove at medium heat.
2. Grate the potatoes and onions into the bowl. Potatoes "leak" water when cut up raw, so drain the bowl just before the next step.
3. Quickly add the eggs, salt, and pepper, and mix well with the potatoes.
4. Drain again. Add the flour, and mix. The mixture should be sticky and heavy like thick oatmeal or chocolate chip cookie dough. If it is too watery, add more flour, and if it is not sticking together well, add another egg.
5. Using the mixing spoon, take a nicely mounded spoonful of the mixture and ease it into the hot oil. Push it flat in the oil, and let it fry. Using your spatula, check the bottom of the latke every 60 to 90 seconds to see if it is golden brown. When it is, flip it over until both sides are golden brown, and remove it to paper towels to let it drain and dry.
6. Repeat step 5 until all of your latke mixture is made, and serve with the sour cream and/or applesauce and/or cinnamon and brown sugar. Yum!

To learn more about Chanukah, take a look at these helpful resources:
Isaacs, Ronald H. *Every Person's Guide to Hanukkah.* Northvale, N.J.: Jason Aronson, 2000.
Wolfson, Ron. *Hanukkah: The Family Guide to Spiritual Celebration.* Woodstock, Vt.: Jewish Lights Publishing, 2001.

- As a college adult, you now have the opportunity to discover a wide variety of Jewish thought, practices, and beliefs through Hillel, other venues in your campus community, and traveling to Israel. Life dictates that we are destined to repeat many things that our parents did, but assuming their Jewish identity is not one of them. You are free to explore, challenge, critique, and modify Judaism to meet your own personal expectations and relationship with it. Feel comfortable experimenting with Jewish practice, knowing that it is adaptable within certain parameters. You should seek the advice of a trusted rabbi for a better understanding of those parameters. At the same time, be mindful that different rabbis understand those parameters in different ways, so you may want to seek the insight of more than one to add to your perspective. Also, be aware that there are outer limits that define those parameters, even in the most liberal branches of Judaism. As an extreme example, believing in Jesus is simply outside the parameters of Judaism, no matter what someone from Jews for Jesus might tell you.

- Finding your own Judaism can only be done through being informed. College offers you the opportunity to equip yourself for Jewish adulthood. Many universities offer Judaic studies courses that allow you to explore Judaism academically and for credit, as well as Hebrew courses. There are adult education courses offered through Hillel, the synagogue movements, and other Jewish venues that allow you to explore the vast areas of Jewish belief and wisdom and that are designed to help you learn at your own level and pace. There are Israel travel and study experiences and summer experiential learning opportunities that allow you to explore specific areas of interest to you and your future. You can even engage in Jewish study on-line! The point is that just as you are preparing yourself academically for an adult life, so should you prepare yourself Jewishly as well. Make educated decisions about your own Judaism. Whether or not you liked the religious school of your childhood, this is a whole different experience. Demand and expect better, and you will love what you learn and the person it helps you to become.

- Do not accept or reject the Jewish denomination you were raised in on the basis of your childhood experience. Often students will assume that the synagogue they grew up in represents an entire denomination of Judaism, and on that basis they generalize anything connected to that denomination. Usually that generalization is incorrect, as it is based not on the theological foundations of that denomination but rather on the quality

If you want to find out more about the various denominations in their own words, check out these websites:
- Reform—http://www.uahc.org
- Conservative—http://www.uscj.org
- Reconstructionist—http://www.jrf.org
- Orthodox—http://www.ou.org

of an individual experience with a particular synagogue. A lousy Reform religious school experience, for example, does not mean that Reform Judaism on the whole has nothing to offer you. Similarly, a wonderful relationship with a Conservative rabbi does not necessarily mean you have a Conservative belief system, and discomfort with a lot of tradition does not mean you cannot identify with Orthodoxy. You owe it to yourself to look beyond the outer trappings often used to judge a synagogue—how much Hebrew they use, use of a musical instrument on Shabbat, whether men and women sit apart—and start to explore what each denomination thinks about God, Torah, and the world at large. Engage rabbis and leaders from each denomination in these discussions, and challenge them with your own questions and concerns. If you are unsure what to ask, a good starter question is "What do you believe happened at Mount Sinai?" Since Mount Sinai is said to be the place where the Torah was given to Moses, this is really a question that gets to the core of one's belief system. The wide range of possible answers reveal a great deal about someone's stance on God, faith, Jewish history, interpretation of sacred texts, and how Judaism is to be lived today. You will be amazed at the breadth of thought that exists in the Jewish community on this one question alone. Feel secure in your exploration process, and do not feel rushed to identify with one particular stream of Jewish thought. Feel free to "hop" between various synagogues and minyans (prayer groups) to experience different ideas and practices and to experiment with a variety of customs and traditions. Time and life experience will help you to determine who you are theologically.

- Just as in politics, there are extremists in religion, and Judaism has its share. There are two particular stripes of extremism often found on campuses. One is the far right. These are Jews who believe that the only true path of Judaism is that of the ultra-Orthodox, and they reject any other viewpoint. It is their purpose on campuses to convince contemporary Jews that they need to embrace a more traditional lifestyle and to reject a contemporary approach to Judaism. These people often have buildings or offices on campuses similar to Hillels and may offer similar programming, but they offer it from only one Jewish perspective and expect a certain amount of conformity to that perspective. People representing these ultra-Orthodox groups are often warm, kind, and well-intentioned people doing what they think is God's expectation of them by "saving" other Jews, but they are extremist in their theology and single-minded in their mission. Engaging

Here is a list of some study programs and their web addresses:
- Beit Midrash Liberal Yeshiva—www.huc.edu/bmaly/
- Kolel: The Adult Centre for Liberal Jewish Learning—www.kolel.org/pages/courses.html
- Institute for Informal Jewish Education—www.brandeis.edu/ige/
- The Brandeis Collegiate Institute—www.thebbi.org/bci www.brandeis-bardin.org
- Pardes Institute of Jewish Studies—www.pardes.org.il
- Hornstein Program in Jewish Communal Service—www.brandeis.edu/jcs
- University of Michigan Program in Jewish Communal Leadership—www.ssw.umich.edu/drachler/
- Jewish Theological Seminary—www.learn.jtsa.edu

Here is a list of a few sites where it is possible to study Judaism on-line:
- UAHC Department of Adult Jewish Growth—www.uahc.org/growth
- Torahnet—www.torahnet.org
- Hillel Jewish Resources—www.hillel.org

For help on dealing with missionaries and cults, talk with your local campus Jewish professional, and hit these websites: Jews for Judaism—http://www.jewsforjudaism.org; and the JCRC Task Force on Missionaries and Cults—http://www.tforce.org. Also, a great book on cults is *A Jewish Response to Cults* by Rabbi Gary Bretton-Granatoor (New York: UAHC Press, 1997).

with them can be difficult and deceptive, and exploring Judaism with them should be done with awareness and perspective. On the other end of the spectrum are Jewish-Christians. These groups go by various names such as Jews for Jesus, Messianic Jews, and Hebrew-Christians. The very idea of these groups is oxymoronic. One cannot be Jewish and Christian at the same time, as Judaism simply does not accept Jesus as the Messiah. The Jewish denominations differ on exactly what if any form a Messiah would take in this world, but all of them agree that a Jewish Messiah cannot be God or any part of God as taught by Christianity. These self-described Jewish-Christian groups can be found on many campuses, and their mission is to "save" Jews by convincing them to accept Jesus as the Messiah. These groups cannot be engaged Jewishly because, despite the Jewish trappings of their rituals, they are not practicing Judaism. Their mission is evangelical—they believe they have a divine requirement to convert Jews to Christianity, and you should be extremely wary of their attempts to dialogue with you "Jewishly." Also keep in mind that despite appearances, the leadership and financing of these groups is generally not Jewish at all, but rather right-wing Christian.

They call them "finals" because when you turn them in, it's FINALLY break!

As you prepare for finals, you probably are also planning your winter break. For many students, especially freshmen, home is the first stop of the break. Unless you live fairly close to home or went home for the High Holy Days or Thanksgiving, winter break is your first chance to go home since you left for college at the beginning of the term. You have been on your own now for several months, determining your own schedule and lifestyle. Don't be surprised if your parents notice little changes that you now take for granted, like your haircut, style of dress, makeup, or food preferences. After all, you have been on your own for a while, and your tastes may be starting to change. You may also interact with them differently, striking up a political science debate with them after the evening news or wondering if your mom's nervous laughter indicates a deeper psychological issue. This of course is because you have been immersing yourself in new thoughts and ideas. Of course, you might also be more aware of things about your parents that you hadn't thought about before, such as why your parents work where they do or how they can accept their lives the way they are now. While it doesn't happen to everyone, and it is not as obvious in commuter student families, this familial distortion is normal during the first visit home. You will all settle back into normalcy once you adjust to the changes. Some families adjust faster than others though, so it is a good idea to consider a few things before you head home for break.

- First and foremost, remember the Jewish concept of honoring your parents. If things get tense with them, keep a cool head. Sit down with them and talk rationally, maturely, and respectfully. Listen as much or more than you speak. Families have patterns in how they fight, and these are often based on events from your childhood or adolescence. Now that you are grown, you can choose not to follow those patterns. Honor your parents with your adult behavior, and ask them to honor you in the same way.

- You've been keeping your own schedule at school, but your parents may still assume you will be adhering to your old curfew while you are at home, especially if you have younger siblings there. Honor your parents by talking over any concerns like that with them before you get home to prevent uncomfortable scenes later. Usually with some advanced discussion, they will let you choose your own hours or be willing to strike an acceptable compromise.

- Don't surprise your family by bringing anyone home unexpectedly. While you may think your new friend or relationship is the greatest, your parents may resent not having any private time with you when they haven't seen you for a term. If the relationship is an intimate one, don't expect that the sleeping arrangements will be the same at your parents' house as they are at school. If there are younger siblings at home, your parents may be concerned about the example you would be setting for your siblings. Even beyond the issue of younger siblings, it may be hard for your parents to accept the fact that their child is in an intimate relationship, especially if you haven't spoken to them about your relationship beforehand. Honor your parents by asking permission first to bring anyone home, and do not be angry if they do not say yes. There will be other chances in the future.

- You may find a different relationship starting to develop with your friends from high school. They have probably been away at school having their own life experiences and are growing and changing just like you. This may be even more apparent with friends who did not leave home. They are having fewer new experiences and are undergoing less change. Some of your friendships will adapt and stay strong, but some of them, without the common bond of high school, will eventually dissipate. As you notice changes, discuss them with those friends with whom you want to stay close and see if they feel the same tension. In Hebrew, a good friend is called a *chaver*. The word *chaver* comes from the root "connect," so literally a *chaver* is someone to whom you are deeply connected. *Chaverim* will talk through life changes and adapt to their new lives. Be sure to keep the friendship fresh by showing interest in their new lives too and learning about their new priorities. *Chaverim* are worth the effort!

- If you plan on traveling over the break, honor your parents by letting them know in advance so that they can plan accordingly. If they plan on your being home and schedule their lives to be with you, then a change in those plans on your part could not only disappoint them but inconvenience them as well. It is best to try and get home for at least part of the break to see them; after all, they are your family. This will make them happy and will make you feel less stressed and guilty. If you want to travel, just strike a compromise with them well in advance, and everyone will be happy.

- Among your travel options will most likely be several opportunities to go to Israel. If you have not been before, you should seriously consider the option. There are several all-expense-paid or heavily subsidized programs for you to go on during the winter break. Going to Israel is not like going to Europe or South America for vacation—this is your Jewish homeland! Even if your family has been in North America for generations, Israel is still the historic and religious homeland of the Jewish people. It is your birthright to visit Israel and to connect yourself with the land and its people. You can tour, go for an academic credit program, study Jewish texts, live on a kibbutz, or do many other things there. The main question from American students tends to be about whether travel to Israel is safe. All organized trips to Israel put safety first and foremost in the agenda. Of course there is an element of risk, but there is in every country in the world. The media has a voyeuristic habit of only showing the worst on television, so what we see of Israel is often an act of terrorism or a Palestinian riot. This is like showing the TV show *Cops* to people from another country and letting them think that is what all of America is like. That just would not be true, and neither is the media's portrayal of Israel. Israel is a beautiful country that is both ancient and modern, and every Jew has a connection to Israel whether he or she knows it or not. Israel will challenge and define you Jewishly, and accept you no matter what kind of Jew you have been or want to be. While you are in school go and discover Israel. If you have been before, go and rediscover it.

Ask your local Hillel staff about winter break travel options to Israel, including programs that offer academic credit, or ask your parents to call your hometown congregation and Jewish federation to inquire about Israel trips. These websites also contain the latest information on travel to Israel, including free trips: http://www.israelexperience.org and http://www.birthrightisrael.org. Either way you will get the information you need for a life-changing experience!

Spring Semester

Zayde was only half-kidding
when he said he went to the University of Life...

Going to college is a life passage that most Jews in America today take for granted. In fact, Jews are among the highest proportionally represented ethnic groups on campus—it is estimated that there are over 400,000 Jewish students on North American campuses today. However, it is only within the last sixty years or so that the campus of our choice has been completely open to us.

Historically, colleges were religious institutions sponsored by a specific church or religious body. The University of Notre Dame in Indiana, for example, is a Catholic-sponsored university, while Baylor University in Texas has Baptist roots. Amherst College trained men for the Christian ministry. At one time it was thought that all education was of a religious nature. During the Middle Ages, it was believed that all one needed to know was found in the Bible or related religious studies.

Jews, seen as "nonbelievers," were not allowed to attend Christian or Islamic universities until the modern era. At the same time, we evolved our own system of education based on the Talmud and have historically valued study as a vehicle to wisdom. As a result, we have always had a relatively high literacy rate despite limited opportunities. Often denied the right to own land or to participate in many professions, in the lands in which we lived, we developed a merchant community with an educated rabbinical class. Jewish merchants traded with Jews of other lands and became renowned for their international business contacts as a result. Rabbis served in a broader capacity than today, working as teachers, judges, advocates, moral authorities, even doctors and matchmakers. Since we could not participate in the national culture, legal system, or social order of the countries in which we lived, we developed our own, based to a high degree on the talmudic legal and social system. Hence, we were a landless nation able to sustain ourselves with varying degrees of contact with the surrounding peoples, and we could take our law and culture with us wherever we went if circumstances dictated that we had to move, which happened frequently throughout history.

Crossing Delancy for Dartmouth:
A *Bissel* History of Jews and Universities

Why Jews value a college education, what it has meant for our past, and what it means for your future and your choice of a major

When the French Revolution occurred at the dawn of the nineteenth century Jewish reality in Western Europe began to shift inextricably. Napoleon became emperor in the wake of the French Revolution, encountering numerous Jewish communities in the lands he conquered. He recognized the economic value of these Jews due to their strong trade links and business skills. He also realized that if he were able to bring the Jews into his new social order, it would be a powerful symbol for the world at large about the benefits of living under French rule. Napoleon therefore convened a "Sanhedrin" in Paris. This was a powerful symbolic move on his part, as the original Sanhedrin was an ancient Jewish legal body that predated the Talmud and was the main governing body for the Jews of its time. Napoleon's Sanhedrin was composed of Jewish leaders from throughout France. He put to them a series of questions that were meant to determine just one thing: were the Jews of France willing to swear loyalty to French law and France over Jewish law and Israel? If so, he was willing to change the law of France to allow them access to all aspects of French society, including the universities, the professions, and land ownership. He gave the Sanhedrin a series of questions to debate and asked them to send a delegation to him with a response. Among the questions were whether the Jews could swear to obey French law first where it conflicted with Jewish law, and could Jews swear a loyalty oath to France and therefore fight in her armies and support her causes? To us living in North America today these may not seem like difficult questions, but to the French Jews of the nineteenth century, these were unheard-of scenarios. Jews had never in history been given such choices or had any prospect of equal citizenship since the destruction of the Second Temple in the first century C.E. The Sanhedrin debated these questions and decided, in almost all instances, that if given the chance they could adapt their laws and culture to be compatible with French society at large. Napoleon therefore changed the laws of France to admit the Jews as citizens under the law with the rights and privileges that entailed, and he applied that law wherever his armies conquered.

Eighteen hundred years of discrimination did not change overnight as a result of Napoleon's actions. As Jews were able to enter the world at large, we were faced with new ideas, new concepts, and new challenges. We have struggled for the last two hundred years with how to adapt to our new surroundings and how to balance our Judaism and our Jewish identities with our national identities. Furthermore, the world has not always welcomed us. Hitler, for example, sent many German Jews to the gas chambers whose families had lived in Germany for generations and who had even fought in the German army in World War I. But the changes instituted by Napoleon had a major impact on Jews and the options available to us.

Waves of Jews immigrated to America in large numbers. The first significant surge of Jewish immigrants was in the years before the Civil War. The next surge came in the 1880s and 1890s, and the latest waves were after World War II and the fall of Communism. Immigrants who arrived in the mid-1800s did not tend to go to college. There was plenty of work for those without a college education, and Jewish merchants from other countries adapted well here. By the 1880s and 1890s though, immigrant families wanted to send their children to college to allow them to advance beyond their parents. The economy was changing, as was the social order, and people knew that education was the key to adapting and succeeding in this changing environment. At the same time, alumni who saw themselves as protectors of cultural values and racial purity controlled many of the best universities, especially the private ones, such as Harvard and Dartmouth. These were largely white Protestants whose families had been in America for many generations, and they believed the immigrants would dilute and demean what they perceived as America's virtues and values. Hence they placed restrictions on who could be admitted to their universities and formalized by quota the number of "others" that these institutions could accept. It was not just Jews who were restricted, but African-Americans, Hispanics, Asians, women, and many other groups. As a result, there was a great demand for public universities that would be supported by the government and open to any academically qualified person. One of the great examples of these universities that helped to educate American Jews out of the immigrant class is the City University of New York (CUNY). It provided quality education for any New York City resident at affordable costs, often on flexible hours and on multiple campuses, so students could work and study at the same time. Thousands upon thousands of the children of Jewish immigrants went to CUNY and from there to success in American society, business, the arts, and politics. Many private institutions were also started to meet this demand, with Brandeis University as the best example in the American Jewish world, and Morehouse College for African-American students.

Gradually, in the twentieth century, American society as a whole began to oppose discrimination of all types and to celebrate diversity, and these restrictions and quotas fell away. Today, a college education is not only the key to a future but is almost a given for every Jewish child who wants one.

Jewish students in the twenty-first century can attend any university they qualify for and can afford. It is easy to take these opportunities for granted. However, it is worth remembering as you walk across your campus that not so long ago your great-grandparents might not have had the same opportunity and that they worked hard so that you could have all of the opportunities you have today.

With that in mind, it is worth factoring your family history into your choice of a major in college. The technological explosion of the last century has caused many students to turn toward technical skill areas such as engineering or computers. The liberal arts are still an important part of an education as well because they provide a good foundation for the complexities of adult life and help develop critical thinking skills. No matter what you choose to study, graduate degrees are strongly encouraged or even required in order to be able to compete in an increasingly sophisticated job market. Thinking Jewishly about your major and course of study can be helpful, if not immediately obvious, and there are some factors you may want to weigh as you formulate your academic plan.

- Jews have a history of family businesses. This comes from a time when we did not have many career options open to us, so it became common for a family to pass a business or at least a trade skill from generation to generation. Are you thinking about a career in a family business? If so, talk with the relevant family members and see what they think about you joining the business in the future. Are they planning to continue the business after they retire? Would they discourage you from joining it? Why or why not? What do they think about you pursuing a related field, and do they recommend a particular course of study? Have they had a happy life in that line of work? Do you think you will have a happy life in that line of work? Be sure also to talk with non-family members in similar businesses to get a neutral perspective. Sometimes it is hard to be objective with your own relatives!

- The same advice applies for any profession you are considering. Seek out people in that field and pick their brains about both their professional and personal lives and choices. Your home congregation can also be a great source of potential mentors in a variety of fields. Speak to your rabbi, cantor, educator, or temple administrator to find a member of the congregation who works in a field that interests you. Learn the ups and downs, and ask for their advice and direction. The more you know, the better decision you will make.

- What do you want to learn besides what you need for your intended career? College is the place to explore those areas you've always been interested in. It is supposed to help round you as an adult as much as train you for a career. What would you like to learn toward that goal? You will have few opportunities in your life again to study something just because it interests you. Do you want to pursue literature, a foreign language, art or music, or even something athletic? Majors are designed to give you a certain amount of elective credits for just such purposes, so take advantage of them!

- Have you considered exploring Jewish topics as part of your studies? There has been a flowering of Judaic studies departments in the last twenty-five years on many college campuses where all sorts of Jewishly related topics can be studied from an academic vantage point. You can study Jewish philosophy, literature, history, politics, anthropology, language, and many other areas for credit, and it will give you an appreciation for your religion and ethnicity that you probably were not mature enough to appreciate when you were in religious school. You can even major and get a Ph.D. in Judaic studies, and there is no "religious" requirement either. You will be amazed at what you can learn too.

- Seriously consider taking Hebrew as a foreign language elective. Hebrew is not only the historic language of the Jewish people, it's the national language of Israel. Most North American Jews learn only enough Hebrew in supplementary education to get through a prayer service. That's the equivalent of teaching someone enough Shakespearean English to read *Romeo and Juliet* (never mind actually comprehending it)—hardly adequate for conversing on the streets of New York. Hebrew is a vibrant, modern language, and learning it can connect you to other Jews in a modern and meaningful way, as well as go a long way toward making the State of Israel feel more like home when you visit. If you can get academic credit to grow Jewishly, why not?

- When you start to narrow down your major and share it with your family, you may be surprised to hear a response from some of them to the effect of "What does a nice Jewish kid like you want to do that for?" That remark is not as flip as it sounds. Remember that we have only been able to pursue what we want academically and professionally for a relatively short period of time. It was not very long ago at all in our historical memory that we were denied the opportunities you are now enjoying. Jews, especially older ones, still feel a cultural insecurity that requires us to optimize our financial and professional options like law or medicine lest we squander them and end up being peddlers again. Therefore a choice of major like forestry or art history or women's studies that seems not to take such an advantage could elicit some uneasy remarks like "Jews don't do that" from other Jews! Understand where they are coming from and use the opportunity to dialogue with your family about why they do or do not value your possible choices of a major. You may be surprised at what you learn about your own family's values and roots as a result.

Mom, what's a "groove thing"?

For some students, college is synonymous with party. Party is synonymous with opportunity, and opportunity is synonymous with sex. Somewhere in the back of everyone's mind is the hope or fantasy that he or she will meet someone with whom there is an opportunity for a sexual relationship. While it used to be the case that there were social systems in place to limit unsupervised contact between people of the opposite sex as well as social pressure to abstain from premarital sex, that is primarily no longer the case. All of that changed during the "sexual revolution" of the '60s and '70s. (Ask your parents about their college social life and see if they blush, fluster, or get some kind of a deer-in-the-headlights look.) Many social and academic figures of the time encouraged people to loosen their moral slipknots and enjoy life more. The revolutionary era gave way to the decade of "me," and it was thought that if it felt good and didn't hurt anyone, you should do it. That included not just sex, but drugs and alcohol as well. People were reacting to many things of concern at the time, including the Vietnam War and the civil rights struggles, and this attitude of openness and experimentation became common on campuses across the country.

Judaism has gone through similar changes of its own. Traditionally, men and women were strictly segregated, women who were not virgins on their wedding day were labeled as such in their *ketubot* (Jewish marriage contract), and most parents taught their children "no *chuppah*, no *shtuppah*." After the sexual revolution though, the restrictions in general society were removed, and Jewish customs regarding sexual interaction became a primary line of defense. However, unless they were self-isolated in traditional Jewish communities that practiced a strict separation of the sexes, Jews were engaging in the same behavior as everyone else.

In the '80s we began to learn that there were repercussions for reckless behavior. Teen and other unwanted pregnancy rates soared, and AIDS appeared on the scene. The divorce rate climbed. Today sex is so common among teenagers that according to research (Alan Guttmacher Institute) 80 percent of teenagers have had sexual intercourse by their twentieth birthday. People know the dangers and risks of such behavior, but that does not seem to be a deterrent, and students on campuses are as sexually

8

Flowers, Candy, and Condoms:

Jewish Sexual Decision Making

Making ethical intimate choices now that you finally have your own place active as ever. So the question arises, what is the Jewish view on sex and how do you know if you are making a sound sexual choice?

You gotta love a religion that makes sex a commandment!

In Judaism, sex is considered one of the most important human behaviors. The very first commandment in the Torah is to be fruitful and multiply (Genesis 1:28). This means that we are supposed to have children and that doing so is a holy act. Sex is seen as more than just a means of bringing children into this world though. Judaism views sex as a means of intimately connecting with a spouse in a holy way. Judaism recognizes that having sex is part of being human and does not see it as sinful, but rather as holy. This doesn't mean that Judaism regards all possible sexual behavior as good and acceptable. Judaism recognizes that our sex drives can be rather troublesome if not satisfied. The human sex drive is thought to be part of the *yetzer hara,* "the evil inclination." The *yetzer hara* includes any temptation to do something wrong we may encounter within ourselves, but since so many temptations are sexually connected, it is commonly used to describe sexual urges. By contrast, we call our moral conscience the *yetzer hatov,* "the good inclination," and it has been traditionally understood that any control we exercise sexually or otherwise is the *yetzer hatov.* So if Judaism does not see sex as sinful, why describe it in terms of good and evil? In Christianity, Good and Evil are opposing forces that do battle through humanity to control them. In Judaism, there are no such opposing forces. God is the only player on the stage. Good is anything we do that is in line with what we understand God's will to be, and evil is anything that transgresses that will. Therefore, the English terms "proper" and "improper" are perhaps more helpful ways to think of sexual distinctions in Judaism, depending on the context of the sexual behavior.

Proper sexual behavior has traditionally been defined as occurring within a monogamous marriage that allows for the possibility of procreation. This derives from the biblical and talmudic perspective in which the family was the means for survival. Children could help tend the crops or the herd, do the chores, contribute to the food stores, defend the family, and eventually care for the elderly parents. When Jews transitioned from farming to being city dwellers and merchants, the result was often large, poor families that could not support themselves. Jewish society created penalties for promiscuity, adultery, and illegitimate children, all of which were the result of two people letting their *yetzer hara* get the best of their *yetzer hatov* outside of the proper social context. Today we are part of a larger society that treats these issues with more tolerance, and in many cases Judaism has come to take a less harsh view on these issues as well. While we may agree from a psychological and sociological perspective that sex has been repressed in society to the point of causing psychological damage, Jewishly we understand that in the proper social context sex should not be repressed at all but rather enjoyed. In the modern world the challenge to Jews is making an ethical determination about what is the proper social context. In no place is it more important to determine that ethic than on the college campus.

Thinking it through before your brain drops into your pants

Sex on campus is so enticing in part because it represents freedom. The idea of doing things you fantasized about with someone new in your life in the privacy of your own room with no parents to contend with can be a real turn-on. It symbolizes adulthood and maturity, and society treats it as a "grown-up" act. You are exercising complete control over your own body with someone else who is doing the same, and it is completely your right to do so. As you well know though, the sex drive is rather impatient. It does not want to wait for fulfillment; it wants some now! That is the *yetzer hara* in classic behavioral mode. You logically know, though, that such behavior without some preparation is reckless and even dangerous and that there are emotional strings attached that your sex drive just doesn't want to notice at critical times. That is your *yetzer hatov* doing its job. And so the tug-of-war of freedom versus responsibility continues. Now is the time to think about your personal ethics and not when that incredibly hot person is sitting next to you in your room. A little forethought now can save you a lot of regret later, whether you choose to turn out the light or not.

- Start with the basics. This is not a childish question. Do you want to wait until you are married or not? Think back to the traditional model of marriage. Sex within marriage was preferable precisely because marriage was a safety net. Our ancestors knew that it is much harder to raise a child or to be sick alone than in a partnership. They even viewed having consensual premarital sex as the equivalent of being married! No matter how good your birth control is, nothing is foolproof, and if you are heterosexual, you run a pregnancy risk every time you engage in sexual behavior. Marriage is no guarantee of a perfect safety net either, but it does offer the safest scenario. How comfortable are you with the odds? Our faith has always valued abstinence for very practical reasons, not because of moral prudishness. Two thousand years of tradition can't be completely wrong, can it?

- If you choose not to wait, what criteria are you using for choosing a sex partner? How well do you know the person? An important Jewish concept is that every person is made in the image of God, so anonymous sex with a drunken pickup or a prostitute would not be a Jewishly acceptable choice. At the same time, sex with someone you do know reasonably well but only desire physically doesn't work Jewishly either. The essence of God in all of us resides in our personalities and intellect, not our bodies, and encounters that are only physical do not fit a Jewish model. In our society today, the idea of depersonalized sex with no obligations or connections beyond the physical level has become normalized. At some level though, sex is not fulfilling if it is consistently just a physical act. You can disconnect your emotions from your body for a while, but you can't do it forever. That does not mean you have to love someone to be sexual with them, but Judaism would encourage having an honest relationship based on mutual trust before knowing someone intimately.

- In the twenty-first century, sex can literally kill you. This is a simple statement of fact. AIDS on campuses today is prevalent, prominent, and real. Unprotected sex can be as fatal today as a bullet to the brain. Judaism values life above all else, and there is no Jewish justification for choosing to engage in premarital sex without using condoms and birth control. There are two separate issues here. Condoms can literally save your life, and children can literally change your life. You owe it to yourself and your partner to protect each other from events for which neither of you is prepared. Judaism traditionally reserves sex for marriage because only in committed life relationships can people be sure of the best chances of mutual and familial support when life events such as children and illness occur. If you are not ready for that kind of a commitment but still think you are ready for sex, you must use appropriate protection for the life, health, and future of both of you.

- Homosexuality is a part of this discussion too. Jewish tradition has viewed homosexuality as an "abomination" forbidden explicitly in the Torah, and Orthodox Judaism still maintains a strict prohibition against it. However, Reform and Reconstructionist Judaism have spoken out on theological grounds that homosexuals are not an "abomination," but rather are fully sanctified people who are biologically oriented by God and not by choice. Both of these movements have made public statements embracing gay and lesbian Jews both as congregants and as Jewish professionals. Conservative Judaism has not embraced the same position to this point, but it has taken a position of narrowing the transgression to homosexual acts and not homosexuals themselves. Many gay and lesbian Jews do not feel free to express or admit to themselves or others their sexual orientation until leaving home and coming to campus. It is often a time of confusion, rebellion, adjustment, and self-acceptance, and can be a challenging time. Many Jewish gays and lesbians are estranged from Judaism, which seems to embrace a traditional heterosexual model, and often assume it has no place for them. Gay and lesbian Jews sometimes also feel no obligation to adhere to Judaism's positions on marriage and monogamy because they would not apply to them. But Judaism's teachings on sexual behavior have as much to teach Jewish gays and lesbians as they do straight Jews. Equally, just as for straight college students, abstinence until a life partner is found is surely the safest option for homosexual students, and protected, monogamous, consensual sex is the next best option. Connecting with a rabbi or other Jewish community leader on campus who can either support or refer you to a support system while you struggle with the very real issues of coming to terms with your sexuality can be both emotionally and spiritually helpful. If you think you cannot find a place within Judaism as a homosexual, think again and seek some help to find your way to an open and accepting Jewish place.

- Regardless of your sexual preference, remember that in Judaism no means no. The Talmud views a man who pursues a woman sexually against her will as a thief. We know today that sexually assaulting someone steals his or her dignity, sense of safety, self-esteem, and sometimes even the ability to love another person securely again. If you are the aggressor, you can be expelled from college for it and even possibly go to jail. Both men and women should seek guidance and advice about sexual assault and date rape from the local campus police, wellness center, women's groups, and student services.

- Remember, even if you choose not to be sexually active, you will hopefully meet someone special with whom you will want to spend quality time when you are not in class. Be sure to use good roommate etiquette when you bring that person home. Respect your roommate's space and privacy. Don't have an overnight guest without checking with your roommate first, and don't monopolize any shared space with your guest. A little courtesy at home can make both your new relationship and your roommate feel at home.

Looking for books on being Jewish and gay? Here are a few recommended resources:
Balka, Christie, and Andy Rose, eds. *On Being Lesbian, Gay, and Jewish.* Boston: Beacon Press, 1991.
Beck, Evelyn Torton, ed. *Nice Jewish Girls: A Lesbian Anthology.* Boston: Beacon Press, 1989.
Elwell, Sue Levi, Rebecca T. Alpert, and Shirley Idelson, eds. *Lesbian Rabbis: The First Generation.* Piscataway, N.J.: Rutgers University Press, 2001.
Raphael, Lev. *Journeys and Arrivals: On Being Gay and Jewish.* Boston: Faber and Faber, 1996.

For resources for Jewish gay, lesbian, bisexual, and transgendered students, surf to http://www.wcgljo.org—the World Congress of Gay and Lesbian Jewish Organizations.

The following list is a sampling of books that explore a variety of perspectives on Judaism and sexuality:
Boteach, Shmuley. *Kosher Sex: A Recipe for Passion and Intimacy.* New York: Doubleday, 2000.
Isaacs, Ronald H. *Every Person's Guide to Jewish Sexuality.* Northvale, N.J.: Jason Aronson, 2000.
Westheimer, Ruth K., and Jonathan Mark. *Heavenly Sex: Sexuality in the Jewish Tradition.* New York: Continuum, 1996.
Yedwab, Paul. *Sex in the Texts.* New York: UAHC Press, 2001.

LET'S GET SERIOUS FOR A MOMENT . . .

Purim arrives in late winter or early spring, and on campuses it is often the biggest Jewish party of the year. One of the most consistent stereotypes of college life is that drugs and alcohol are free-flowing and commonly used by everyone. While the amounts and types of chemicals used on campuses today may have changed since your parents went to college, that stereotype is not completely off base. On most campuses today, social drinking is still the norm, and drugs of various types are available if sought. You have probably gotten more "just say no" lectures and "don't drink and drive" talks than there are words in this book. You know the risks and dangers of use and abuse of alcohol and drugs, and you know they could kill you or get you into serious legal trouble. Since you know all of that, it isn't necessary to repeat it here. Instead, a discussion of Purim provides a good opportunity to look at the Jewish perspective on these issues.

Jewish tradition has always been fairly liberal when it comes to the drinking of wine. In the ancient world, wine was the drink of choice for most people in no small part because there were not a lot of beverage options back then that were safe to drink. Since Judaism views eating as a religious act in which we consume food that God provided for us through nature, we have always said a blessing over the wine we drink at a meal. Our ancestors knew that wine had an intoxicating effect as well, and at times it became mandated to feel those effects as part of religious celebration. The most obvious example is Purim. While for kids Purim is a bit like Halloween, with costumes, carnivals, and lots of treats, for adults it is more like Mardi Gras, with lots of drinking, dancing, and nuttiness. The talmudic rule is that on Purim you are supposed to drink until you cannot tell the difference between the villain Haman and the hero Mordecai in the Esther story. Jews have taken this rule literally, and many a Jew has gone to hear the *M'gillah* read the next morning with a serious hangover. While this rule has always been meant as a means of enhancing the celebration, it was established at a time in history when much less was understood about the dangers of alcohol. Today alcohol is more plentiful than in talmudic times. It is mass-produced in factories in a wide variety of forms that are often much more potent than the wine of the ancient world, and it is sold cheaply. Because it is easier to obtain

Purim and Pubs: The Mitzvot of Responsibility

Understanding why *L'chayim* means "To life" and how to keep it that way

Purim is the holiday that celebrates the salvation of the Jews of ancient Persia from a plot to wipe them out by the prime minister, Haman, through the bravery of a teenage Jewish queen named Esther. For more on the story and meaning of Purim, read the Book of Esther in the Bible.

For help in planning for Purim, see the "High Holiday Initiative Program Pack on Purim" by Kesher. The packet can be obtained by contacting Kesher, either by e-mailing to Kesher@uahc.org or by calling 212–650–4070.

and more plentiful, today there is a higher rate of alcohol poisoning and alcohol-related fatalities than our ancestors ever had to deal with. There were no automobiles in talmudic times, so no one was concerned with the dangers of drinking and driving. There were few laws about public or underage intoxication then, and they knew far less about the long-term dangers of alcohol abuse than we do today. In short, holding up Purim as an example of Judaism's views on celebratory drinking is using an outdated and naive guideline.

A popular myth in the Jewish community is that alcoholism is not a Jewish problem. This myth purports that because we have such a cultural comfort level with alcohol due to our religious use of it, Jews only overindulge on religious occasions, having become accustomed as a community to moderation. Unfortunately, this is a false assumption. Jewish statistics of alcoholism in North America are as high as any other subgroup of society. We have no monopoly on sobriety and self-control. Our history does not accurately inform our present. Going to celebrate at a Purim party can be a great way to mark the holiday. But if you want to be realistic about drinking responsibly at the celebration, then you have to be realistic about drinking responsibly the whole year round.

While we have no cultural history regarding drugs, our tradition speaks forcefully about taking care of our bodies, as they are gifts from God. For that reason, we can partake of almost any chemical for medicinal reasons if it is reasonably believed it can heal us. At the same time, we are forbidden from taking anything that has no medicinal purpose, especially if it could harm us. This includes tobacco. There is no complicated lesson here. If you are going to smoke, snort, inject, or swallow something that you think might give you some kind of a desired rush but has no other purpose and in fact is potentially dangerous, then Judaism does not condone your use of it. Period. At the same time, if you are already beyond that point and in fact may be dealing with an addiction, then you have a Jewishly motivated reason to seek treatment and save your life. There are even Jewish treatment and support organizations. *Purim* literally means "lots," as in lottery. Don't play chance games with your life. If you need help, just ask.

For more on Judaism and chemical abuse and addiction and where to get help for it, surf to http://www.jacsweb.org—Jewish Alcoholics, Chemical Dependents and Significant Others. Also check out *Twelve Steps to Recovery* by Rabbi Kerry Olitzky and Dr. Stuart Copans (Woodstock, Vt.: Jewish Lights Publishing, 1992) and *Addictive Thinking: Understanding Self-Deception* by Rabbi Abraham J. Twerski, M.D. (Center City, Minn.: Hazelden, 1997) http://www.hazeldenbookplace.org.

Matzah au gratin . . . yum, yum, gimme some!

Springtime. The birds are chirping, the trees are budding, and the matzah balls cannot be far behind. That greatest of spring holidays, Passover, shows up around the middle of the spring semester, often around spring break time. Passover is the most commonly celebrated holiday among American Jews. It is the American Jewish cultural equivalent to Thanksgiving dinner; even Jews who work on Yom Kippur usually find their way to a seder. It is the quintessential family experience, and everyone going to a seder is seeking a connection to their homes and communities, even if they are among strangers. Nowhere is this more clear than on campus. Campus seders are a lot like campus High Holy Day services in that they consist of customs similar but not exactly identical to the ones you know from home, and that those attending are not usually with their families either and are seeking community at this time of year. The differences are that by the time this holiday arrives, you have usually established a group of friends so that you are not alone when you go to a seder. Also, this holiday lasts eight days and requires some choices about observance that you did not have to consider when you lived in your parents' home.

Passover commemorates our enslavement in Egypt and how God liberated us. Celebrating Passover is a sign of our continual covenantal relationship with God. It permeates not only our religious theology but our cultural norms as well. Some Jewish businesses and institutions close for Passover week, and the idea of removing *chameitz* (food products with yeast or other food items unacceptable for Passover consumption) from the home often becomes an almost obsessive priority. Some Jews who do not regularly keep kosher have a set of Passover dishes and make an attempt to abstain from *chameitz* for the week in order to be "kosher for Passover." You may have memories of hosting seders at your home, boxing up non-Passover foods like bread or pastas and putting them away for the week, or changing dishes and silverware. To whatever degree your family observed Passover, they could do so because they had a home of their own. Passover is a home-based holiday, closely tied to what and how we eat. On campus though, you often are not living in a home of your own in which to observe the holiday, and that can put a real crimp in how you celebrate it.

What If the Dining Hall Doesn't Serve Gefilte Fish?: Doing Passover on Campus

How to find the foods, the Jews, and the initiative to make a meaningful Passover on campus

Orthodox and Conservative Judaism observe Passover for eight days while Reform Judaism observes it for seven days. The Torah specifies seven days, but tradition has interpreted this to apply only to Jews living in Israel. An extra day is observed by Jews outside of Israel in part as an acknowledgment that Jews who live outside Israel are still technically in exile and in part due to the vagaries of the ancient calendrical system. Reform Jews follow the Israeli practice because they do not believe that Jews who freely choose to live outside of Israel can still be seen as in exile.

The good news is that Passover on campus is quite doable with some advanced planning. It is easiest to think of it on two levels: seder and other meals. Seder is a communal ritual meal that tells the Passover story. Every family celebrates seder differently, and every family has customs and stories about seders that help make it a special occasion. Because most family seders consist of a major feast and a table service led by the eldest or most Jewishly literate member of the family, most students think they have to go somewhere else for seder instead of their own college homes. In truth, participating in a seder on campus may be the easiest option. Hillels, Jewish student unions, and even residence halls on campuses with large Jewish populations generally host a community seder for those who are unable to go home. They will provide Passover food, Haggadot, seder leaders, and everything needed for a fine seder. On campuses lacking these resources due to a small Jewish population, students can often go to a seder at a Jewish faculty member's home or to a local synagogue seder. Students often forget to find one until hours before seder starts and room is always being made at the campus seder table to hold just one more, but planning ahead never hurts.

Turn a dorm desk chair into a recliner!

Ready-made campus seders are great options. But don't overlook the possibility of hosting your own seder. Seders like Bubbe used to make are a wonderful idea, but not always practical. However, a little improvisation can make for a great home seder. First, find a couple of Jewish students who are going to be on campus for seder. If you are not sure how, then post a simple sign in several places inviting anyone interested in a student-led seder to e-mail you. You do not even have to list your name, just your e-mail address. Jews will recognize the word "seder" and will know what it means, so anyone interested will contact you. Also ask your Hillel or Jewish student union to post the notice on their list serve or website or in their building. They will usually be glad to help. Also post it at fraternities or sororities that have Jewish membership. Word of mouth will spread, and soon enough you should have a few people.

Decide ahead of time where you want to hold the seder so you know how much room you will have available. Residence hall meeting rooms, Greek house dining rooms, student center dining rooms, apartments, even a smaller room at the Hillel are possible and accessible if you ask. Make sure you reserve the room well in advance.

Once you have your group, determine together just how *pesadich* (kosher for Passover) you want the seder to be. If you all want a strictly kosher-for-Passover meal, you may be able to purchase precooked meals from Hillel or a kosher caterer in town that you can just heat and serve. You can also *kasher* (make kosher) a kitchen for Passover. This is time-consuming but not impossible. Ask a local rabbi or other Jewish professional for help, or ask a rabbi on the website of the movement you mutually agree to follow for the purposes of the seder. Remember, there are varying degrees of acceptability as to what constitutes kosher for Passover. Many Jews are comfortable only abstaining from symbolic foods like bread during Passover and do not observe strict kosher-for-Passover diets or kitchens. Therefore you need to discuss this so everyone is comfortable, and someone will have to assume the responsibility of learning what is involved in meeting the group's needs. Remember that you will need a kitchen that can be prepared for Passover. Often your Hillel will let you borrow theirs or help arrange the use of one for you. You will also need to decide how you are keeping Passover during the rest of the week too. Hillel or the cafeterias often arrange Passover meals for the entire week, but if you want to prepare your own food for the week in your kitchen, it can be done more easily than you would probably expect.

One mistake to avoid is believing that Passover food has to be purchased in a box or can. Many Jews reach for the familiar orange box of *pesadich* muffin mix or stuffing just because they know it is kosher for Passover, even if they would not eat muffins or stuffing the rest of the year!! Lots of acceptable food can be prepared from scratch using fresh foods such as vegetables, fruits, meats, eggs, and dairy without resorting to processed or premade items. Your Hillel or other campus Jewish source will usually be glad to help you order the right Passover foods for your needs if they are not easily accessible to you. This includes wine too. Most kosher wine is kosher for Passover, and you can use kosher-for-Passover grape juice if you do not want to use wine. You don't have to use the sweet syrupy stuff either, unless that is what you like; there are lots of decent kosher-for-Passover wines out there if you want to splurge and live a little. Ask at Hillel or a local kosher food purveyor or wine seller for help in finding them.

If you decide to cook for the seder, there are some wonderful cookbooks with simple basic recipes you can follow even if you have minimal cooking experience. What many North American Jews assume are Passover recipes, like tzimmes or kishka, are actually Ashkenazic or European recipes passed down in families. In fact, there are a wide variety of types of

---

Jews whose families come from Europe tend to be more restricted in the types of foods they can eat during Passover than Jews whose families come from the Middle East or Africa. Items that European Jews don't eat are called *kitniyot* and include foods like corn, rice, beans, and their by-products among others. Be sure to ask your guests what their family customs are regarding Passover foods.

If you choose to keep a strictly observant kosher-for-Passover kitchen, be aware that there are certain Passover rules about meat and dairy. A rabbi can easily explain these, and often simple over-the-counter products can suffice. If you buy matzah meal to replace bread crumbs, matzah flour to replace flour, and potato starch you will have the starch substitutes for most recipes. Also buy some cheap cookware, knives, utensils, and a cutting board that you will use for Passover only. In terms of shopping and preparation, it is easier to decide to eat only milk or only meat meals for Passover, in addition to pareve meals (containing neither dairy nor meat products).

For good Passover recipes, see:
Amster, Linda, ed. *The New York Times Passover Cookbook: More Than 200 Holiday Recipes from Top Chefs and Writers.* New York: William Morrow, 1999.
Nathan, Joan. *The Jewish Holiday Kitchen.* New York: Schocken Books, 1988.
Rauchwerger, Lisa. *Chocolate Chip Challah and Other Twists on the Jewish Holiday Table.* New York: UAHC Press, 1999.

For a quick and easy Passover side dish, go to the latke recipe in the section on Chanukah. Simply substitute matzah meal for the flour, pour the mixture into a 9x13-inch oiled baking dish, and pop it into an oven preheated to 350 degrees. Bake 35 minutes or until it is golden brown on top and you can poke it with a toothpick that comes out clean. Voila! Pesach potato kugel!

There are literally hundreds of Haggadot, but the following are good ones to consider for a campus seder:

Bronstein, Herbert. *A Passover Haggadah.* New York: CCAR Press, 1994.

Dishon, David, and Noam Zion. *A Different Night.* Israel: Shalom Hartman Institute, 1997.

Elwell, Sue Levi. *The Open Door: A New Haggadah.* New York: CCAR Press, 2002.

Levit, Joy, and Michael Strassfeld, eds. *A Night of Questions: A Passover Haggadah.* Elkins Park, Pa.: Reconstructionist Press, 2000.

Rabinowicz, Rachel Anne. *Passover Haggadah: The Feast of Freedom.* New York: The Rabbinical Assembly, 1982.

For fun though, just type "Haggadah" into your web search engine to see what you find!

For additional help in planning for Passover, see the "High Holiday Initiative Program Pack" on Passover provided by Kesher. It can be obtained by either e-mailing to Kesher@uahc.org or calling 212–650–4070.

Passover food from Jewish communities around the world. Whether your family is European in origin or from Asian or African origins determines the customs you grew up with. Tradition says that you only eat during Passover what your family customs allow, but not every Jewish family today feels bound to that tradition. With your group, determine what your parameters are for your seder. Also, ask your families for good Passover recipes. Tell them about your space, time, and other limitations and see what they can suggest. Aunt Tilly or Uncle Herman might have just the thing to make your seder special!

Once you have the food and the people taken care of, you need only worry about the seder rituals themselves. Seders were traditionally times for dialogue, sharing, and storytelling for the entire family. Somewhere along the way, they became highly ritualized and Jews felt obligated to read the Haggadah word for word without allowing for innovations. Today, Jews are learning to celebrate the seder again. There are an enormous variety of Haggadot out there, so you can find one that you like—you don't have to use your parents' version.

The seder is wonderful in that it is so adaptable to the times without losing its essential story of our liberation from Egypt. It has become quite common on campuses today to hold seders with specific focuses such as women's seders, Black-Jewish freedom seders, GLBT seders, vegetarian seders, or even seders that are defined by the participants such as graduate student seders or seders by academic major or age group. Here either a prewritten Haggadah can be purchased, or a standard one can be adapted to meet the needs of the group. There are even CD-ROM versions that can be edited on your computer or downloaded from websites. One or a few people must be willing to plan the seder rituals, but with a little guidance from someone who has led a seder before, it is quite simple and rewarding. Parts can be assigned ahead of time, and a musical person can lead the songs.

The bottom line is that if you choose to make seder and Passover more than just a boring ritual, it can be done, and done enjoyably. By doing so, you have not only chosen to make your college Passover better, but taught yourself skills to make Passover for yourself throughout your life. Of course going to a campus community seder is a good experience, and getting home for Passover is the best of all, but Passover on your campus is possible if you are willing to give it a try.

Mourning in a meaningful way

If you ever attend services at Hillel, take a moment and look around when the Mourner's *Kaddish* is recited. You may notice two differences from your home congregation. First, there will probably not be a *yahrzeit* (memorial) list that is read to mark the anniversaries that week of the deaths of congregants or their family members, as in a typical synagogue. Second, you will probably see few, if any, students stand to recite the *Kaddish*. The reason for this difference is that the vast majority of college students do not experience the death of a close loved one while they are in school. Unlike your grandparents' generation, which experienced World War II and the Holocaust, or your parents' generation, which experienced the Vietnam War, you have lived in a relatively crisis-free time in history where war has not claimed large numbers of people from our society. At the same time, medical science has significantly raised the age of mortality as well as lowered the death rate due to disease. As a result, college-age students often do not encounter the death of a close loved one until well after graduation. Nonetheless, it is always a reality of life that death could take someone from you unexpectedly while you are at school, and you may find yourself trying to cope with the reality and finality of death as well as struggling to mourn your loss in a Jewishly meaningful way.

Judaism requires that we mourn only for immediate family—parents, siblings, spouses, and children. This is not to say that we are not to grieve in the case of the death of someone else close to us. It simply means that we are not considered official mourners. This is an ancient limitation that comes from a time of high death rates due to illness, war, poor hygiene, and lack of medical knowledge. There was simply too much death in the world to permit more regular mourning restrictions, or else daily life would have been constantly interrupted. Since most students today are not yet married, the first two categories are usually of more concern. However, it is in fact more common for students to experience the death of a grandparent than a parent or sibling. And due to AIDS, drug abuse, and drunk driving, it is sadly not entirely unheard of to lose a good friend either. Despite not being official mourners in these cases, Judaism acknowledges that these relationships can be just as meaningful as those traditionally mourned, and sometimes even

A Late-Night Phone Call: "Honey, We've Got Some Bad News..."

Dealing with death away from home and what you can Jewishly do to mourn more so, and that these losses can be just as painful. Judaism therefore allows for, though does not require, expressive mourning rituals to be utilized for these nontraditional categories of relationships as well. The extent of these rituals for nontraditional relationships can depend on the denomination you follow and even the rabbi you consult, so it is important to seek guidance when trying to cope with loss in a Jewishly appropriate way.

Jewish tradition has many rituals and rules regarding mourning. While not all of these may be meaningful to you, it is helpful to know what they are, as they are designed both to help you cope with loss and help you transition back into regular life. Jewish mourning is defined by a seven-day period of semi-seclusion with family and the abstention from regular activities such as school or work. This period is called shivah. This is followed by a thirty-day period called sh'loshim, during which you go back to work or school, but traditionally abstain from anything socially pleasurable such as parties, dates, or movies. During both shivah and sh'loshim, men traditionally do not shave or cut their hair as a sign of mourning, and mourners attend daily prayer services to say the Mourner's Kaddish. After sh'loshim, the next eleven months are pretty much back to normal, although people tend not to get married or conduct other major joyous occasions and some choose to say Kaddish daily. They also go to synagogue at least every Shabbat to recite the Mourner's Kaddish. Generally, the headstone is laid after eleven months with a ceremony called an unveiling, and that ends the Jewish mourning process except for saying Kaddish on the anniversary of the loved one's death each year.

No matter what your connection is, when someone close to you dies it is a loss. Here are some suggestions for how you can work through your grief in the campus Jewish community.

- If you have lost an immediate family member, try to get home for the funeral and shivah. It will be much more comforting to you in the long run to grieve with your family and to bury your dead than to stay away. Do not worry about your schoolwork, as most campuses have bereavement policies that will allow you to make up work and exams at a later point. Have a friend apprise the dean of students or academic affairs about the situation so that he or she will be able to help. Ask this friend to be your contact person, and be sure to check in with him or her from home when you are able. Most airlines have a reduced rate for people going to funerals, so don't assume you can't afford to go home. When you call for reservations, ask the airline for the special rate and how to obtain it.

Travel agents can be helpful with this as well. The airline will usually want some information or proof regarding the funeral like an obituary or death notice to be sure that you are not trying to defraud them, as well as proof of a relationship to the deceased. Don't be angered by this, as people do try to obtain these rates under false pretenses. The paperwork can be cumbersome, but the rates can make a difference in helping you get home at this difficult time.

- If you are able to make it to the funeral, participate to the extent that you are able to based on your own emotional strength and comfort with the tradition. Do not be afraid to turn to your family for support. Allow yourself to be the child or the grandchild if you have lost a parent or grandparent. Your memories may be childhood memories, and you may feel the loss with a child's pain. Do not hesitate to allow yourself that; you are entitled. Also feel free to talk about your loss with others. Being stoic is not a Jewish virtue—Jews believe in communal sharing and supporting mourners. It can help to talk about your pain and also to share memories of the deceased's life.

- Do not be afraid to seek counseling back on campus to cope with the pain and loss. If your feelings start to interfere with your daily life beyond a reasonable period of time, seek help in dealing with it. Judaism values life and living above all, and if mourning prevents you from doing so, then you are mandated to seek the help you need to move on with your life.

- Shivah differs from family to family and denomination to denomination. Some families observe the traditional full seven days, and others observe only three according to a rule allowing the period to be cut short if it would severely impair business or, in a student's case, school. Consult a rabbi or Jewish professional you trust about this if you are unsure what is right for you. Once back on campus, determine if you wish to say *Kaddish* daily, as is traditional for mourners. If so, ask your Hillel where there is a daily prayer service you can attend. If the only available service is Orthodox, a woman may not be allowed to say *Kaddish*, although some will. Ask before you attend if this is important to you. If you cannot find a daily service, consider asking Hillel or some Jewish friends to put one together with you. A minyan (a group of ten people, men and women in the non-Orthodox denominations) is required to say the Mourner's *Kaddish*. It can be done anywhere at any time, although evenings are often the most convenient. It is a real mitzvah to help someone make a

There are some wonderful books to help Jews cope with loss. Some good ones are:

Bremer, Anne. *Mourning & Mitzvah: A Guided Journal for Walking the Mourner's Path Through Grief to Healing.* Woodstock, Vt.: Jewish Lights Publishing, 1993.

Lamm, Maurice. *The Jewish Way in Death and Mourning.* Middle Village, N.Y.: Jonathan David Publishers, 2000.

Sonsino, Rifat, and Daniel B. Syme. *What Happens After I Die? Jewish Views of Life After Death.* New York: UAHC Press, 1990.

minyan for saying the Mourner's *Kaddish*. When asked, most Jewish students will rise to the occasion.

- If you should have to miss the funeral, consider having a memorial service of your own with your friends. Organize it on or near the time and date of the funeral, and ask some friends to come. It can be as simple as your sharing a few memories of your loved one, reading a few psalms, and then saying the Mourner's *Kaddish* together. Someone might be willing to put a service together for you too if asked, and again, Jewish professionals on campus are there to help. You may observe shivah if you want, although it will be harder to do so by yourself, both emotionally and from a practical perspective. If you would like, ask your family to arrange a phone time for you with the rabbi officiating at the funeral so you can share some thoughts about your loved one for the eulogy. That way you can share your feelings with your family and friends even if you are not there.

- Jews do not send flowers to funerals, as they are seen as a sign of life and therefore are felt to be inappropriate at a time of death. There is also a sense that money is better spent on the living rather than the dead. For this reason, it is customary to make charitable donations in someone's memory. Donations are seen as living memorials, while flowers, like us, are perishable. Consider giving to or raising money for a cause that was important to your loved one or doing some community service in your loved one's memory. We also have a tradition of dedicating something we have learned to someone's memory, so perhaps you could read a new Jewish text or even set an academic accomplishment as a goal to honor the deceased. These are things you can actively do on campus to help you grieve and heal.

- Unlike many other religious traditions, Judaism does not embrace definite ideas about heaven or hell. While there are a variety of Jewish perspectives on the afterlife, in general we hold that God cares for us after we pass. The focus in Judaism, therefore, is on the earthly life of our loved ones and what they accomplished here. The rest we leave in God's hands. We gain strength from their earthly life and memory and know that the lessons we learned from their lives are a legacy that will help us continue to grow.

Springtime?! Spring me outta here!

Unbelievable as it may seem, once Passover has passed, you are on your way to finishing your first year of college! Spring finals are only weeks away. As you are already well aware, there are different ways to study. There are "methodical" studiers who follow formulaic ratios of hours in class to hours of preparation for class at a steady pace. There are "surfing" studiers who tend to peak and wane like the tide in their studying according to the quiz schedule of a class. There are "so what" studiers who never seem to feel the need to do it at all, and there are the "planned cram" studiers who wait until the pressure of finals is on to actually open the books. There are study tips in chapter 6 that are equally applicable for spring finals too, but don't be shocked if you find yourself doing a few all-nighters regardless of how well you have studied over the year. Springtime on campus is usually an active period of student life, especially if you are on a campus that gets hit by a lot of cold winter weather. Big events like Spring Fling and Greek Week tend to be held, which offer a lot of fun distraction, and you may already be planning ahead for the summer. It's also the time when students start concentrating on tans, fitness, and flirtations because...well, it's spring. The point is, you may not be as focused on the books as you were toward the end of fall because you are ready for something new and different. Enjoy yourself—just don't allow short-term fun to interfere with your long-term academic goals. This may involve an all-nighter or two for test preparation, so just be prepared to accommodate some time for sleep after the exam!

Sinai express: Open all night and we deliver!

Judaism has an all-nighter tradition of its own. The holiday of Shavuot falls around the end of the spring term, fifty days after the first day of Passover. It was originally a biblical festival that culminated the harvest period after Passover. When Jews became predominantly city dwellers rather than farmers, the Rabbis of the Talmud reinterpreted the significance of Shavuot into a commemoration of receiving the Torah at Mount Sinai. They determined that the date of Shavuot coincided with Moses coming down the mountain. The custom developed that we wait all night with anticipation for the dawn that marks the day that we received the law. This is traditionally marked by what

Pulling an All-Nighter for God:

What Actually Happened at Sinai?

Shavuot as an opportunity to tackle the heavy theological stuff like revelation, covenant, and the whole Messiah thing

The Rabbis, also known as the Sages, is a reference to the numerous rabbinic voices in both the Talmud and the vast collection of biblical commentary called midrash.

is called a *Tikkun Leil Shavuot,* literally "a perfecting of the evening of Shavuot," by engaging in Jewish studies all night to pass the time until dawn. For many Jews, the custom has been shortened from all night long to a late-evening event, so you may not have ever had the chance to participate in an all-night Shavuot study session. On campuses though, where students are night owls anyway, this can be a really great opportunity to do some Jewish exploration without interfering with classes, social events, or other plans.

Shavuot is a great time to ask the big question that is at the root of the Jewish denominational differences in theology: What exactly did happen on Mount Sinai? This is no small or esoteric question because it is the central dividing point in Jewish theology, one that bound us together through many generations and has separated us in modern times. It is a core piece of what makes each synagogue the type of place that it is, because much of what it stands for is connected to this issue. It is a key question for any adult Jew to wrestle with as you determine what type of a Jew you want to become.

Tradition holds that God gave Moses the whole Torah verbally on Mount Sinai and he transcribed it into the scrolls that we have today. Tradition also maintains that Moses was given a series of verbal instructions that were passed down to the leaders of each time period to apply to their time, until the Rabbis compiled these cumulative instructions into the Talmud. Talmud is therefore called the Oral Torah and is seen by traditional Jews as second only to the Torah itself. The idea of the Torah and Talmud coming in some form directly from God is called "revelation" because God is believed to have revealed all of this to Moses and continued revelation in different forms until the end of the rabbinic period, when direct revelation ceased. The idea of divine revelation was critical in the development of Judaism because it is the underlying belief behind Jewish law and practices. In other words, if it was God who said something should be done a certain way, it carries much more weight than if it was just some person's idea.

The discrepancies of interpretation of revelation begin with the Torah itself. The Torah states that God gave Moses the tablets that contained the Ten Commandments and the Torah (Exodus 20), but the word *Torah* in the Bible is understood to mean "holy law" and not necessarily the five books of the Bible that we call the Torah today. All holy law is considered Torah, including the Talmud, or the Oral Torah. The idea that the Torah referred to in Exodus 20 is the scrolls that we call Torah today is not stated explicitly in the Bible but rather comes from the Rabbis of the Talmud. Tradition says that they knew that the meaning of the word *Torah* referred to the scrolls containing the first five books of the Bible because they possessed the oral revelation that had come through the generations from Moses that told them this. However, Jews at least as far back as Maimonides have questioned this understanding and challenged the notion of revelation as the tradition has understood it.

Did I say that?!

If the rabbinic definition of Torah is not historically accurate, in other words, if God did not dictate the first five books of the Bible to Moses for him to carry down the mountain to the people, then the question is, what exactly in the Torah is actually from God? After all, if the Torah was transcribed at a later date in history by humans, it is subject to human editing and error. In other words, it would be something like a game of telephone. Remember that game? You sat in a group and one person whispered a sentence to the person next to him or her. The sentence had to pass through the whole group until it came back to the originator. More often than not, it would come back different than what was originated because people along the way had misunderstood it or misheard it or edited it in the transmission. That is the basic challenge to the idea of the Torah as a complete, perfect document from God to Moses to us. Modern science and technology have added to this issue by raising questions based on archaeology, linguistics, carbon dating, and other modern disciplines. Clearly there is far more to this topic than can be tackled here, but the point is that this initial question has led to a variety of answers as to how to believe and observe Jewishly in the modern era.

While it would take several chapters just to explain the theological nuances of the different denominations of Judaism, it is important to understand how each group views the question of revelation. The founders of Reform Judaism, who lived in the eighteenth and nineteenth centuries, when science and reason were changing the way people viewed the world, were uncomfortable with the nonrational nature of the traditional understanding of revelation. Reform theology therefore developed the position that the rabbis could not have received a complete revelation from Moses through the ages. They questioned the idea that the revelation on Sinai included the whole of the first five books of the Bible. An important Reform principle is that in an age of democracy and individual rights and freedoms, rabbis cannot make decisions for a community of individuals but rather can better serve by teaching and empowering the individual Jew to make religious ritual and life

For a snapshot of Reform's theological development over the last three centuries, go to http://www.ccarnet.org/platforms/. Also check out *Reform Judaism Reader: North American Documents*, edited by Michael Meyer and W. Gunther Plaut (New York: UAHC Press, 1999).

For more on Conservative Judaism, go to http://www.uscj.org.

For a fuller look at Reconstructionist theology, go to http://www.rrc.edu/reconstructionism/.

decisions for themselves, even if it counters long-held Jewish traditions. The individual Jew can experience revelation as much as any rabbi or communal leader, and so God engages individuals in their decision making to the extent that the individual allows it. However, while the founders of Reform Judaism viewed much of Jewish law and practice as irrational, since it was based on the irrational belief in divine revelation, today's Reform Jews have begun to reconnect to Jewish law and practice. The individual Jew is free to seek personal connection and meaning in rituals and traditions and to reinterpret them in a dynamic new way.

Conservative theology differs in its understanding of the place of the rabbinic tradition. While also questioning the divine origins of the Torah and the Talmud, Conservative Judaism maintains that the rabbinic tradition has held great weight throughout the ages and cannot be discounted on an individual basis without a loss of integrity and validity of the law to the community itself. Therefore the Conservative rabbinate accepts a concept of Jewish legal decision making within a modern context that is as binding as traditional Jewish law upon the community. They also embrace the idea of a continual revelation to rabbis who engage in the process of making legal decisions for the Jewish community so that they are as engaged in divine action as the Rabbis of Talmud were for their communities.

The Reconstructionist branch of Judaism is the stream most informed by modern scientific experience and attributes much of its theological influence to sociology and anthropology. It views Judaism as a culture that has evolved through time, as have other cultures on the planet. Revelation is seen as a process of human ethical evolution as the culture progresses through history and the concept of God in the culture changes to manifest the ethical ideals of any given period. A God that has spoken directly to humanity with instructions for living throughout the ages is only an ethical construct for a period of our history that required it, and we have today evolved beyond it. Therefore, religious decisions today are communal decisions, and Reconstructionist communities operate within a communal process of understanding and governance.

While the focus of this book is for students from non-Orthodox Jewish backgrounds, it's important to point out that Orthodoxy is a vibrant and viable Jewish movement. The name "Orthodox" is actually a Greek word that roughly translates as "correct belief," obviously a point of contention with the other streams of Judaism. Orthodoxy promotes the belief that the Torah is the true and pure word of God, that the commandments contained within are inviolate, and that the Talmud holds the primary, divinely initiated understanding of those commandments, which cannot be countered or changed except by strictly observed rules of rabbinic interpretation. Contrary to the assumption of many, Orthodoxy is neither "original" Judaism, nor monolithic. It too has changed, divided, and adapted to the times. There are a variety of groups that affiliate under the theological rubric of Orthodoxy, all struggling in their own way to balance the experiences of the modern world with their understanding of God's commandments as timeless and eternally binding.

North America's largest Orthodox organization is the Orthodox Union. To learn more about it and Orthodox Judaism in general, go to http://www.ou.org.

Judaism has a wide variety of viewpoints about revelation. However, even if the traditional teachings about what happened at Mount Sinai are questioned, the Torah and the Talmud themselves still are the root of all Jewish theology and practice. Shavuot, therefore, is a very valuable holiday for all Jews, not only traditional Jews, because it is centered around text study. Even if we disagree as to the origins of our key texts, we are united in our value of them. More importantly, Jews cannot truly comprehend their own theological positions without wrestling and dialoguing with the tradition. Through that process, the story of Sinai can be meaningful for all of us, even as a metaphor, and we can all feel a sense of commandedness even if we question whether the texts themselves are of divine origin. Judaic studies classes try to lay out the academic theories about the origins and preservation of our texts and theologies, but they do not tackle faith, as that is not a scientifically provable fact. Opportunities for discussion about truth, faith, and theology therefore have to be sought out. Shavuot is an excellent opportunity for this type of study and search. Here are some suggestions as to how you can have an enjoyable Shavuot study experience:

- The easiest method is to go to a text study on the evening of Shavuot at a local Hillel or synagogue. Call first to see what type of study is being offered.

- Another option might be to plan your own study. There are many options and formats to use that do not require much preparation or background. Ask some Jewish friends to participate in a one-time study session with you. A traditional text for study on Shavuot is the Book of Ruth, because Ruth is seen as a prime example of the righteous convert who accepts Jewish law and tradition. Consider splitting your group into men and women. Have each group read and discuss the book as a single-sex group and then come together to share insights as a mixed group. You will be amazed at how men and women can read the same text differently and

Midrash is rabbinic commentary on the Bible that attempts to fill in the blanks of a biblical story or to read between the lines. It does not replace the Bible but rather accentuates it by giving additional possibilities. You can really come to appreciate the world of Jewish thought by spending a few hours reading midrash!

uniquely! Or pick a favorite biblical story to study, and discuss what you like or don't like about it and what you feel is the truth or message of the story. Ask a local rabbi or Jewish campus professional for some accessible midrash to study.

- If you are not comfortable or feel rusty with Jewish texts such as Bible or Talmud, consider tackling some twentieth-century Jewish writers such as Abraham Joshua Heschel, Mordecai Kaplan, or Lawrence Kushner, in particular:

  Heschel, Abraham Joshua. *The Sabbath*. New York: Farrar, Straus, and Giroux, 1999.

  Kaplan, Mordecai. *Judaism as a Civilization: Toward a Reconstruction of American-Jewish Life*. Philadelphia: Jewish Publication Society, 1994.

  Kushner, Lawrence. *Eyes Remade for Wonder: A Lawrence Kushner Reader*. Woodstock, Vt.: Jewish Lights Publishing, 1998.

  They all write in clear discernible English and in a modern tone. They can be read individually or as a group. Other books that offer accessible, engaging introductions to many of these ideas and texts are the following:

  Holtz, Barry W. *Finding Our Way: Jewish Texts and the Lives We Lead Today*. New York: Schocken Books, 1993.

  Sonsino, Rifat, and Daniel B. Syme. *Finding God: Selected Responses*. New York: UAHC press, 2002.

  Telushkin, Joseph. *Jewish Literacy: The Most Important Things to Know About the Jewish Religion, Its People, and Its History*. New York: William Morrow, 1991.

- Assign people to find a Jewish text of any kind that is of interest to them and have them prepare it for discussion. Ask each person to take an hour, and make sure to mix it up in terms of topics. You can learn as much about each other by what topics you pick as by what you say in the discussions.

- As an alternative to reading, consider renting a video on an interesting ethical issue and holding a discussion afterwards. Two favorites for this are the Woody Allen movie *Crimes and Misdemeanors* and a wonderful film called *The Quarrel*.

- Like most Jewish holidays, there is a food tradition associated with Shavuot. Dairy foods are customarily eaten on Shavuot because legend tells us that when the Jews returned to their tents after receiving the Torah, they were too famished to wait for a meat meal to be cooked, so they ate whatever dairy foods were at hand. Ashkenazic Jews eat blintzes because

The Union of American Hebrew Congregations has also put together packets for Shavuot study, which include a video, texts, and discussion questions. The collection, entitled *Tikkun Leil Shavuot: The Voice Still Speaks,* can be obtained from the UAHC Press at www.uahcpress.com.

two of them side by side resemble the Ten Commandments. Feel free to grab a few pizzas for your study, or bring the fixings for an ice-cream sundae bar for a campus-style celebration. Noshing and talking—this is the quintessential Jewish holiday!

- Don't feel you have to stay up all night if you think setting that as a goal will discourage you or others. Do just as much as you think you can and feel satisfied with the effort. Remember though, while not everyone will stay up until dawn, it is worth the try if you have not seen a sunrise in a while. The power of seeing the first rays of morning light after a night of debate and dialogue on the essence of Judaism is really incredible, and the connection with God through reciting the *Sh'ma* out loud when you see the sunrise is intense. Shavuot—it's worth the effort.

If not now, when?

With spring finals comes the end of the year, and you'll probably be taking the summer off for a well-deserved break. Many students travel over the summer, but lots of students get summer jobs. Should you go for the best-paying jobs, especially if you need the money to apply toward school? Should you take the job that will be the most fun, because you will have so little time in your adult life for just enjoying yourself? Should you take a position that will benefit your future career plans even if you have to do it as a volunteer? Or should you find something that has intrinsic value beyond your finances or career?

Think about dedicating part or all of your summer to a social action project. Judaism places great value on the idea of *tikkun olam,* "repairing the world." We are partners with God in caring for and maintaining the world. The world is incomplete, but we can perfect it if we try hard enough. This idea has led to the Jewish emphasis on social action, that by each of us going the extra mile to do the right thing, we can help repair the world. *Tikkun olam* is also connected to the Jewish value of *tzedek,* "justice." Judaism teaches that all of us are entitled to justice and obligated to pursue it. That is what makes *tzedakah* different than charity. While *tzedakah* is commonly translated as "charity," they are not the same. Whereas charity, from the latin word *caritas,* implies something that you do by choice because you want to, Jews give *tzedakah* or engage in *tikkun olam* because it is part of our obligation as Jews. There is not necessarily any "feel good" aspect to *tikkun olam* or *tzedek;* we are obligated to do the right thing regardless of how difficult it may be or how it may make us feel.

Judaism has a long history of philanthropy and communal service. This stems in part from times in our history where we were denied access to communal services because of religious discrimination. It was thus incumbent upon us to raise the funds and provide the services internally to care for those in need in our communities. Once in North America, we found ourselves in a country that still could discriminate against us based on our faith but that also allowed us to be financially successful according to our abilities. We therefore continued our philanthropic work within the Jewish community and created state-of-the-art institutions such as hospitals, homes for the aged, and schools

Summer Vacation: Repairing the World While Working on Your Tan

Considering social action as a summer job

that became among the best in the country. We also learned from our history of discrimination to help others who were being discriminated against by breaking down old barriers and building new relationships. As Jews became even more financially successful over time, they began to give to general communal charities as well as Jewish ones. Today it is as common for Jews to be major donors to the United Way and the local symphony or museum as to the United Jewish Communities or JCC.

As we have grown in affluence, we have increasingly become a culture that gives money rather than personal time to our *tzedakah* work. What has gotten lost in this idea of *tzedakah* is the equally valuable idea of *g'milut chasidim*, "acts of loving-kindness." Jews are commanded to engage in personal actions that assist others as much as we are commanded to give money to those in need. For some time this idea looked like it might be lost among college students. Students who lived in a strong economy for most of their lives, who knew no real enemies or threats to their country, who knew only a strong and successful Israel, and who saw the innovation of technologies such as the Internet that bring the world to them rather than forcing them into it were not as involved in helping others as past generations of students had been. Without that empathy and understanding of those in need beyond themselves, college students run the risk of becoming a generation whose leadership has few real ethical or moral values to apply to their decision-making process. However, on campuses today, due in part to changes in the world and the economy, there is a resurgence of *g'milut chasidim* projects and programs designed to connect students to the needs of the world at large.

College students have begun to embrace the idea of social action not just on campus but off it as well. It is now common for colleges to sponsor campus-wide community service days, to have offices devoted to connecting students to community service options, or even to give credit for community service work as an incentive to break out of the comfort zone and help someone in need. The Jewish student community has been at the forefront of these efforts and has taken advantage not just of opportunities during the school year but of summer opportunities as well. Today there are numerous programs that are coordinated by or in partnership with the Jewish community to provide opportunities for *tikkun olam* both in this country and around the world. For example, Hillels across the country are engaged in communal service initiatives called *Tzedek* Hillel, and organizations such as the National Jewish Coalition for Literacy and American Jewish World

Service are creating opportunities for real social change in communities and countries in need.

Tikkun olam is no longer understood as just helping those who are less fortunate than us. Judaism also understands it as political activity within the democratic process to fight for the needs of society at large and to advocate for those who cannot speak for themselves. Time and energy given to local, national, or international political action in a fight for social and legal equalities are an extension of the values of social action as well. This includes Israel as well as North America or anywhere else in the world. We are commanded to perfect this world, as Adam was commanded on our behalf to be its steward, and we cannot do that with a checkbook alone, however well-intentioned that check may be. We must do more and do it personally, because only when we witness injustice ourselves can we value and strive for justice, *tzedek,* as we are commanded to do. So if your summer plans are not made yet, remember that there are only a few obligation-free times left in your life during which you can take a few weeks off to engage in something personally meaningful like social action. If you want to do the right thing, the best idea is to do it now while you have the time. After all, remember what Maimonides said: If I am not for myself, who will be for me? If not now, when?

There are dozens and dozens of social action summer opportunities that can be found through your campus social action office, local Hillel, and community service programs. Here are just a few Jewish programs in the United States worth checking out:
American Jewish World Service: http://www.ajws.org;
AVODAH—The Jewish Service Corps: http://www.avodah.net;
Coalition on the Environment and Jewish Life (COEJL): http://www.coejl.org;
MAZON: A Jewish Response to Hunger: http://www.shamash.org/soc-action/mazon/;
Machon Kaplan of the Religious Action Center of Reform Judaism: http://www.rac.org;
Socialaction.com: http://www.socialaction.com;
Ziv Tzedakah Fund: http://www.ziv.org.

Another great way of serving the Jewish community is to work in a Jewish summer camp! It's a real opportunity to affect the lives of children for the future while having fun and making some money too. For a list of Jewish camps around the country, go to http://www.jewishcamping.org or contact the summer camp division of your movement directly.

14 Final Thoughts

Well, there you have it—Jewish college life in a nutshell. You'll soon find though that campus life is ever changing, and new experiences and opportunities are always coming up. You will grow from adolescence into adulthood during the next few years, and you'll mature Jewishly as well. Remember one key point as you encounter the facts of life that will challenge you Jewishly as well as personally: Don't be afraid to ask questions! The resources in this book are great places to start, but with thousands of years of Jewish history and culture behind us, they are only the beginning. There is an old adage that for every action there is a blessing, and for every question there is a Jewish answer. May your life be full of actions and questions, and may you always pursue blessings and answers!

Shabbat and Holiday Blessings

Shabbat Candlelighting

Baruch atah Adonai, Eloheinu

melech haolam, asher

kid'shanu b'mitzvotav v'tzivanu

l'hadlik ner shel Shabbat.

בָּרוּךְ אַתָּה יי אֱלֹהֵינוּ
מֶלֶךְ הָעוֹלָם, אֲשֶׁר
קִדְּשָׁנוּ בְּמִצְוֹתָיו וְצִוָּנוּ
לְהַדְלִיק נֵר שֶׁל שַׁבָּת.

We praise You, Eternal God, Sovereign of the universe: You hallow us with mitzvot, and command us to kindle the lights of Shabbat.

> May we be blessed with Shabbat joy.
> May we be blessed with Shabbat peace.
> May we be blessed with Shabbat light.

Kiddush for Shabbat Evening

Wine and grape juice are equally "fruit of the vine."

Hold the cup and say:

"Six days shall you labor and do all your work, but the seventh day is consecrated to the Eternal One, your God." With the fruit of the vine, our symbol of joy, we celebrate this sacred day, on which cares and sorrows fade from our minds. We give thanks for life and its blessings, for work and rest, for home and love and friendship. On Shabbat, eternal sign of creation, we rejoice that we are created in the Image of God.

Va-y'chulu hashamayim v'haaretz

v'chol tz'vaam, va-y'chal Elohim

bayom hash'vi-i m'lachto

asher asah, va-yishbot bayom

hash'vi-i mikol m'lachto asher

asah. Va-y'varech Elohim et yom

וַיְכֻלּוּ הַשָּׁמַיִם וְהָאָרֶץ
וְכָל־צְבָאָם: וַיְכַל אֱלֹהִים
בַּיּוֹם הַשְּׁבִיעִי מְלַאכְתּוֹ
אֲשֶׁר עָשָׂה וַיִּשְׁבֹּת בַּיּוֹם
הַשְּׁבִיעִי מִכָּל־מְלַאכְתּוֹ אֲשֶׁר
עָשָׂה: וַיְבָרֶךְ אֱלֹהִים אֶת־יוֹם

Appendix

<table>
<tr>
<td>

hash'vi-i va-y'kadeish oto, ki vo

shavat mikol m'lachto asher

bara Elohim laasot.

</td>
<td dir="rtl">

הַשְּׁבִיעִי וַיְקַדֵּשׁ אֹתוֹ כִּי בוֹ
שָׁבַת מִכָּל־מְלַאכְתּוֹ אֲשֶׁר־
בָּרָא אֱלֹהִים לַעֲשׂוֹת:

</td>
</tr>
</table>

Now the whole universe—sky, earth, and all their array—was completed. With the seventh day God ended the work of creation, resting on the seventh day, with all the work completed. Then God blessed the seventh day and sanctified it, this day having completed the work of creation.

<table>
<tr>
<td>

Baruch atah Adonai, Eloheinu

melech haolam, borei

p'ri hagafen.

</td>
<td dir="rtl">

בָּרוּךְ אַתָּה יי אֱלֹהֵינוּ
מֶלֶךְ הָעוֹלָם, בּוֹרֵא
פְּרִי הַגָּפֶן.

</td>
</tr>
<tr>
<td>

Baruch atah Adonai, Eloheinu

melech haolam, asher kid'shanu

b'mitzvotav v'ratza vanu, v'Shabbat

kod'sho b'ahavah uv'ratzon

hinchilanu, zikaron l'maaseih

v'reishit. Ki hu yom t'chilah

l'mikra-ei kodesh, zeicher

litziat Mitzrayim. Ki vanu

vacharta v'otanu kidashta mikol

haamim, v'shabbat kodsh'cha

b'ahavah uv'ratzon hinchaltanu.

Baruch atah Adonai, m'kadeish

hashabbat.

</td>
<td dir="rtl">

בָּרוּךְ אַתָּה יי אֱלֹהֵינוּ
מֶלֶךְ הָעוֹלָם, אֲשֶׁר קִדְּשָׁנוּ
בְּמִצְוֹתָיו וְרָצָה בָנוּ, וְשַׁבַּת
קָדְשׁוֹ בְּאַהֲבָה וּבְרָצוֹן
הִנְחִילָנוּ, זִכָּרוֹן לְמַעֲשֵׂה
בְרֵאשִׁית. כִּי הוּא יוֹם תְּחִלָּה
לְמִקְרָאֵי קֹדֶשׁ, זֵכֶר
לִיצִיאַת מִצְרָיִם. כִּי־בָנוּ
בָחַרְתָּ וְאוֹתָנוּ קִדַּשְׁתָּ מִכָּל־
הָעַמִּים, וְשַׁבַּת קָדְשְׁךָ
בְּאַהֲבָה וּבְרָצוֹן הִנְחַלְתָּנוּ.
בָּרוּךְ אַתָּה יי מְקַדֵּשׁ
הַשַּׁבָּת.

</td>
</tr>
</table>

We praise You, Eternal God, Sovereign of the universe, Creator of the fruit of the vine.

We praise You, Eternal God, Sovereign of the universe: You call us to holiness with the mitzvah of Shabbat: the sign of Your love, a reminder of Your creative work, and of our liberation from Egyptian bondage: our day of days. On Shabbat especially, we hearken to Your call to serve You as a holy people. We praise You, O God, for the holiness of Shabbat.

Before partaking of food

This blessing is to be said over a piece of bread.

Baruch atah Adonai, Eloheinu

melech haolam, hamotzi

lechem min haaretz.

בָּרוּךְ אַתָּה יי אֱלֹהֵינוּ
מֶלֶךְ הָעוֹלָם, הַמּוֹצִיא
לֶחֶם מִן הָאָרֶץ.

We praise You, Eternal god, Sovereign of the universe, for You cause bread to come forth from the earth.

Kiddush for Shabbat Morning

It is customary to recite the following before the midday meal.
Wine and grape juice are equally "fruit of the vine."

Hold the cup and say:

V'shamru v'nei Yisrael et

haShabbat, laasot et haShabbat

l'dorotam, b'rit olam. Beini

uvein b'nei Yisrael ot hi

l'olam, ki sheishet yamim asah

Adonai et hashamayim v'et

haaretz, uvayom hash'vi-i

shavat va-yinafash.

וְשָׁמְרוּ בְנֵי־יִשְׂרָאֵל אֶת־
הַשַּׁבָּת, לַעֲשׂוֹת אֶת־הַשַּׁבָּת
לְדֹרֹתָם בְּרִית עוֹלָם. בֵּינִי
וּבֵין בְּנֵי יִשְׂרָאֵל אוֹת הִוא
לְעֹלָם, כִּי־שֵׁשֶׁת יָמִים עָשָׂה
יהוה אֶת־הַשָּׁמַיִם וְאֶת־
הָאָרֶץ, וּבַיּוֹם הַשְּׁבִיעִי
שָׁבַת וַיִּנָּפַשׁ.

The people of Israel shall keep the Sabbath, observing the Sabbath in every generation as a covenant for all time. It is a sign between Me and the people of Israel forever. For in six days the Eternal God made heaven and earth, but on the seventh day God rested and was refreshed.

Al kein beirach Adonai et yom
haShabbat va-y'kad'sheihu.

עַל־כֵּן בֵּרַךְ יהוה אֶת־יוֹם
הַשַּׁבָּת וַיְקַדְּשֵׁהוּ.

Therefore the Eternal One blessed the seventh day and called it holy.

Baruch atah Adonai, Eloheinu
melech haolam, borei p'ri
hagafen.

בָּרוּךְ אַתָּה יי אֱלֹהֵינוּ
מֶלֶךְ הָעוֹלָם, בּוֹרֵא פְּרִי
הַגָּפֶן.

We praise You, Eternal God, Sovereign of the universe, Creator of the fruit of the vine.

Before partaking of food

Baruch atah Adonai, Eloheinu
melech haolam, hamotzi
lechem min haaretz.

בָּרוּךְ אַתָּה יי אֱלֹהֵינוּ
מֶלֶךְ הָעוֹלָם, הַמּוֹצִיא
לֶחֶם מִן הָאָרֶץ.

We praise You, Eternal God, Sovereign of the universe, for You cause bread to come forth from the earth.

Havdalah Blessings

The leader raises the cup of wine or grape juice and says:

Baruch atah Adonai, Eloheinu
melech haolam, borei p'ri
hagafen.

בָּרוּךְ אַתָּה יי אֱלֹהֵינוּ
מֶלֶךְ הָעוֹלָם, בּוֹרֵא פְּרִי
הַגָּפֶן.

We praise You, Eternal God, Sovereign of the universe, Creator of the fruit of the vine.

The leader holds up the spice box and says:

Baruch atah Adonai, Eloheinu
melech haolam, borei minei
v'samim.

בָּרוּךְ אַתָּה יי אֱלֹהֵינוּ
מֶלֶךְ הָעוֹלָם, בּוֹרֵא מִינֵי
בְשָׂמִים.

We praise You, Eternal God, Sovereign of the universe, Creator of the world's spices.

The spice box is circulated and all present inhale its fragrance.

The leader holds up the candle and says:

Baruch atah Adonai, Eloheinu
melech haolam, borei m'orei
ha-eish.

בָּרוּךְ אַתָּה יי אֱלֹהֵינוּ
מֶלֶךְ הָעוֹלָם, בּוֹרֵא מְאוֹרֵי
הָאֵשׁ.

We praise You, Eternal God, Sovereign of the universe, Creator of fire.

The candle is held high as the leader says:

בָּרוּךְ אַתָּה יי אֱלֹהֵינוּ מֶלֶךְ הָעוֹלָם, הַמַּבְדִּיל בֵּין קֹדֶשׁ לְחוֹל,
בֵּין אוֹר לְחֹשֶׁךְ, בֵּין יִשְׂרָאֵל לָעַמִּים, בֵּין יוֹם הַשְּׁבִיעִי לְשֵׁשֶׁת
יְמֵי הַמַּעֲשֶׂה.

Baruch atah Adonai, Eloheinu melech haolam, hamavdil bein kodesh
l'chol, bein or l'choshech, bein Yisrael laamim, bein yom hash'vi-i
l'sheishet y'mei hamaaseh.

We praise You, Eternal God, Sovereign of the universe: You make distinctions, teaching us to distinguish the commonplace from the holy; You create light and darkness, Israel and the nations, the seventh day of rest and the six days of labor.

בָּרוּךְ אַתָּה יי הַמַּבְדִּיל בֵּין קֹדֶשׁ לְחוֹל.

Baruch atah Adonai hamavdil bein kodesh l'chol.

We praise You, O God: You call us to distinguish the commonplace from the holy.

All present sip from the cup.

The candle is extinguished by immersing it in the cup.

We give thanks for the Sabbath day now ending. We are grateful for its many blessings: for peace and joy, rest for the body, and refreshment for the soul. May something of its meaning remain with us as we enter the new week, lifting all that we do to a higher plane, and inspiring us to work with new heart for the coming of the day of redemption from every form of oppression. Of this redemption the prophet Elijah is a symbol:

אֵלִיָּהוּ הַנָּבִיא, אֵלִיָּהוּ הַתִּשְׁבִּי,

Eliyahu hanavi, Eliyahu hatishbi;

אֵלִיָּהוּ, אֵלִיָּהוּ, אֵלִיָּהוּ הַגִּלְעָדִי.

Eliyahu, Eliyahu, Eliyahu hagiladi.

בִּמְהֵרָה בְיָמֵינוּ, יָבֹא אֵלֵינוּ;

Bim'heirah v'yameinu, yavo eileinu;

עִם מָשִׁיחַ בֶּן דָּוִד, עִם מָשִׁיחַ בֶּן דָּוִד.

im Mashi-ach ben David, im Mashi-ach ben David.

אֵלִיָּהוּ הַנָּבִיא ...

Eliyahu hanavi ...

שָׁבוּעַ טוֹב ...

Shavua tov, shavua tov, shavua tov, shavua tov.

A good week, a week of peace;
may gladness reign and light increase.

Festival *Kiddush*

On all occasions—hold the cup and say:

Baruch atah Adonai, Eloheinu   בָּרוּךְ אַתָּה יי אֱלֹהֵינוּ

melech haolam, borei p'ri   מֶלֶךְ הָעוֹלָם, בּוֹרֵא פְּרִי

hagafen.   הַגָּפֶן.

We praise You, Eternal God, Sovereign of the universe, Creator of the fruit of the vine.

Baruch atah Adonai, Eloheinu   בָּרוּךְ אַתָּה יי אֱלֹהֵינוּ

melech haolam, asher bachar   מֶלֶךְ הָעוֹלָם, אֲשֶׁר בָּחַר

banu mikol am, v'rom'manu   בָּנוּ מִכָּל־עָם, וְרוֹמְמָנוּ

mikol lashon, v'kid'shanu   מִכָּל־לָשׁוֹן, וְקִדְּשָׁנוּ

b'mitzvotav. Vatiten lanu, Adonai	בְּמִצְוֹתָיו. וַתִּתֶּן לָנוּ, יְיָ
Eloheinu, b'ahavah (shabbatot	אֱלֹהֵינוּ, בְּאַהֲבָה [שַׁבָּתוֹת
lim'nucha u-) moadim l'simchah,	לִמְנוּחָה וּ] מוֹעֲדִים לְשִׂמְחָה,
chagim uz'manim l'sason, et yom	חַגִּים וּזְמַנִּים לְשָׂשׂוֹן [אֶת־יוֹם
(haShabbat hazeh v'et yom)	הַשַּׁבָּת הַזֶּה וְאֶת־יוֹם]
• Chag hasukkot hazeh,	• חַג הַסֻּכּוֹת הַזֶּה,
z'man simchateinu,	זְמַן שִׂמְחָתֵנוּ,
• hash'mi-ni chag haatzeret	• הַשְּׁמִינִי חַג הָעֲצֶרֶת
hazeh, z'man simchateinu,	הַזֶּה, זְמַן שִׂמְחָתֵנוּ,
• chag hamatzot hazeh,	• חַג הַמַּצּוֹת הַזֶּה,
z'man cheiruteinu,	זְמַן חֵרוּתֵנוּ,
• chag hashavuot hazeh,	• חַג הַשָּׁבוּעוֹת הַזֶּה,
z'man matan torateinu,	זְמַן מַתַּן תּוֹרָתֵנוּ,
mikra kodesh, zeicher litziat	מִקְרָא קֹדֶשׁ, זֵכֶר לִיצִיאַת
Mitzrayim. Ki vanu vacharta	מִצְרָיִם. כִּי־בָנוּ בָחַרְתָּ
v'otanu kidashta mikol	וְאוֹתָנוּ קִדַּשְׁתָּ מִכָּל־
haamim, (v'shabbat u-) moadei	הָעַמִּים, [וְשַׁבָּת וּ] מוֹעֲדֵי
kodsh'cha (b'ahavah uv'ratzon,)	קָדְשֶׁךָ [בְּאַהֲבָה וּבְרָצוֹן,]
b'simchah uv'sason hinchaltanu.	בְּשִׂמְחָה וּבְשָׂשׂוֹן הִנְחַלְתָּנוּ.
Baruch atah Adonai, m'kadeish	בָּרוּךְ אַתָּה יְיָ מְקַדֵּשׁ
(hashabbat v') Yisrael	[הַשַּׁבָּת וְ] יִשְׂרָאֵל
v'haz'manim.	וְהַזְּמַנִּים.

Eternal God, You call us to Your service and hallow us with mitzvot. In Your love You have given us (the Sabbath and its rest,) festive times and seasons, together with their joys. They are sacred meeting-days, reminders of our liberation from Egyptian bondage.

We praise You, O God, for these days sacred to Israel.

The following blessing is not recited on the last day of Pesach:

Baruch atah Adonai, Eloheinu

melech haolam, shehecheyanu,

v'kiy'manu, v'higianu lazman hazeh

בָּרוּךְ אַתָּה יי אֱלֹהֵינוּ
מֶלֶךְ הָעוֹלָם, שֶׁהֶחֱיָנוּ
וְקִיְּמָנוּ וְהִגִּיעָנוּ לַזְּמַן הַזֶּה.

We praise You, Eternal god, Sovereign of the universe, for giving us life, for sustaining us, and for enabling us to reach this season.

On Sukkot

On Sukkot, the following is added:

Baruch atah Adonai, Eloheinu

melech haolam, asher

kid'shanu b'mitzvotav

v'tzivanu leisheiv basukah.

בָּרוּךְ אַתָּה יי אֱלֹהֵינוּ
מֶלֶךְ הָעוֹלָם, אֲשֶׁר
קִדְּשָׁנוּ בְּמִצְוֹתָיו
וְצִוָּנוּ לֵישֵׁב בַּסֻּכָּה.

We praise You, Eternal God, Sovereign of the universe: You hallow us with Your mitzvot and command us to celebrate in the sukkah.

Mourner's Kaddish

יִתְגַּדַּל וְיִתְקַדַּשׁ שְׁמֵהּ רַבָּא בְּעָלְמָא דִי־בְרָא כִרְעוּתֵהּ, וְיַמְלִיךְ מַלְכוּתֵהּ בְּחַיֵּיכוֹן וּבְיוֹמֵיכוֹן וּבְחַיֵּי דְכָל־בֵּית יִשְׂרָאֵל, בַּעֲגָלָא וּבִזְמַן קָרִיב, וְאִמְרוּ: אָמֵן.

Yitgadal v'yitkadash sh'meih raba b'alma di v'ra chiruteih, v'yamlich malchuteih b'chayeichon uv'yomeichon uv'chayei d'chol beit Yisrael, baagala uvizman kariv, v'imru: Amen.

יְהֵא שְׁמֵהּ רַבָּא מְבָרַךְ לְעָלַם וּלְעָלְמֵי עָלְמַיָּא.

Y'hei sh'meih raba m'varach l'alam ul'almei almaya.

יִתְבָּרַךְ וְיִשְׁתַּבַּח וְיִתְפָּאַר וְיִתְרוֹמַם וְיִתְנַשֵּׂא וְיִתְהַדָּר וְיִתְעַלֶּה וְיִתְהַלָּל שְׁמֵהּ דְּקוּדְשָׁא, בְּרִיךְ הוּא,

Yitbarach v'yishtabach v'yitpaar, v'yitromam, v'yitnasei, v'yithadar, v'yitaleh, v'yithalal sh'meih d'kud'sha, b'rich hu,

לְעֵלָּא מִן־כָּל־בִּרְכָתָא וְשִׁירָתָא, תֻּשְׁבְּחָתָא וְנֶחֱמָתָא דַּאֲמִירָן בְּעָלְמָא, וְאִמְרוּ: אָמֵן.

l'eila min kol birchata v'shirata, tushb'chata v'nechemata daamiran b'alma, v'imru: Amen.

יְהֵא שְׁלָמָא רַבָּא מִן־שְׁמַיָּא וְחַיִּים עָלֵינוּ וְעַל־כָּל־יִשְׂרָאֵל, וְאִמְרוּ: אָמֵן.

Y'hei sh'lama raba min sh'maya v'chayim, aleinu v'al kol Yisrael, v'imru: Amen.

עֹשֶׂה שָׁלוֹם בִּמְרוֹמָיו, הוּא יַעֲשֶׂה שָׁלוֹם עָלֵינוּ וְעַל־כָּל־יִשְׂרָאֵל, וְאִמְרוּ: אָמֵן.

Oseh shalom bimromav, hu yaaseh shalom aleinu v'al kol Yisrael, v'imru: Amen.

Magnified and sanctified be the great name of the One by whose will the world was created. May God's rule become effective in our lives, and in the life of the whole House of Israel. May it be so soon, and let us say:

Amen. May God's great name be praised to all eternity.

Blessed and praised; glorified, exalted, and extolled; lauded, honored, and acclaimed be the name of the Holy One, who is ever to be praised, though far above the eulogies and songs of praise and consolation that human lips can utter; and let us say: Amen.

May great peace descend from heaven, and abundant life be granted, to us and all Israel; and let us say: Amen.

May the Most High, Source of perfect peace, grant peace to us, to all Israel, and to all the world.

91

Four Perspectives on Jewish Denominations on Campus

Conservative Judaism

Rabbi Bruce Bromberg Seltzer, Jewish Theological Seminary of America, 2000
Duke University Freeman Center for Jewish Life

Conservative Judaism traces its roots to the end of the last century, when it began as a way to conserve traditional Judaism from the changes of Reform Judaism. It views Jewish law (halachah) and tradition as engaging and interacting with modern life, changing gradually to reflect the times. More stays the same than is changed (the Hebrew name of the movement is *Masorti,* meaning "traditional").

One primary value is pluralism: there may be more than one Conservative position about an issue of Jewish law. Pluralism is instituted through legal opinions made by a movement-wide rabbinic board and implemented by decisions by a community's rabbi and by individual Conservative Jews, who determine their own practice. This leads to problems of identity. Conservative Judaism appears not to represent any single position (and is simply a midpoint between Reform and Orthodoxy), since members of a community may hold more than one position and still define themselves as Conservative. Another primary value is using modern critical methods to augment traditional methods of studying our sacred texts and history.

Individuals may define themselves as Conservative Jews because of synagogue affiliation or because of ideology or practice. Identification based on practice would include some of the following: Shabbat and holiday observance, the laws of kashrut, prayer, and Torah study, though the level of observance varies among communities and individuals. Ideological Conservative Jews have usually been participants in the movement's youth programs (Camp Ramah; its youth group, United Synagogue Youth) or have attended Conservative Solomon Schechter day schools. Conservative Jews are often active and vocal members of campus Hillels in addition to the Conservative college group, Koach. The Conservative Yeshiva provides an engaging and serious alternative for Conservative Jews who desire to dedicate time during or after college to Torah study in a Conservative environment.

In college, I increasingly identified with the Conservative Movement through working at Camp Ramah and teaching at the local synagogue.

I began to observe Shabbat and kashrut and decided to become a rabbi. The pluralistic nature of Conservative Judaism appealed to me because it allowed a commitment to halachah with room for personal expression. I find inspiration in studying the texts of our tradition using traditional techniques and modern tools of study and infusing Jewish practice with spirituality and meaning. Its adaptable nature, combined with a commitment to tradition, makes Conservative Judaism a vibrant and meaningful way to be Jewish on the college campus.

Orthodox Judaism

Rabbi Hyim Shafner
Rabbi Isaac Elchonon Theological Seminary of Yeshiva University, 1995
Washington University Hillel

What's the one thing you think you know about Orthodox Judaism? Come on, say it, we all know... THE SHEET! There we go, we put it out there. Well friends, it's a myth. So complete a myth that the Talmud (our two-thousand-year-old book of Jewish law) says that when a wife and husband have sex they must be completely nude so that their flesh can touch in intimacy. Well, in my experience as a college campus rabbi who is Orthodox, there is only one other thing everyone seems to know about Orthodox Jews—that they like to have sex on Friday night because it is a double mitzvah, and actually, that one is true.

For Orthodox Jews, Shabbat is a very sacred, very central time. We have sex on Shabbat both to fulfill the mitzvah of pleasure (oneg) that one is commanded to have on Shabbat and, on a more mystical level, as a symbol of the unification of the Divine with the physical world, which according to Kabbalah (Jewish mysticism) happens on Shabbat. In fact, if I had to point to one central thing in the life of an Orthodox Jew, it is Shabbat. A day of rest so complete, a day so set aside from the rest of the weekdays, that we use no electricity, car, or telephone for twenty-four hours. Shabbat, for the Orthodox Jew, is spent in prayer, eating with family, spirituality, Torah study, and community.

Let me dispel one other myth: all Orthodox Jews wear black hats and long black coats, even in the summertime. In fact, there are lots of different kinds of observant Orthodox Jews. Many Chasidic Orthodox Jews do dress that way. (By the way, Chasidic Jews are different from regular Orthodox Jews in a few ways. They stress the mystical sides of Judaism more, they have a particular Chasidic rabbi they follow who is traced back to the Baal Shem Tov, the first seventeenth-century Chasidic master, and they feel so connected to him they tend to dress like he did.) But most Orthodox Jews do not.

The average Orthodox student you might meet on your college campus would probably look a lot like you. You might run into Orthodox students in the student center or at Hillel or in a class. They could be dressed in jeans, shorts, blue shirt, white shirt, anything. So, how will you know they are Orthodox? Simple. The men will wear a *kippah* or a head covering of some kind (in college often a baseball hat) all the time. They may have some white strings called *tzitzit* peeking out from their belts. These strings are actually the fringes of a small *tallit* (prayer shawl) that most Orthodox (and some Conservative and Reform) men wear all the time under their shirts, in order to keep the Torah's commandment to the Jewish people of putting fringes on a four-cornered garment (Numbers 15:38–39). If it is an Orthodox woman you meet, over time you may notice that her shirts have sleeves even in the summer and her skirts tend to be a little longer than most. All this is in keeping with the Jewish laws of modesty.

The most important thing to remember is that a college campus Jewish community is the only place where you will have the opportunity to explore and get to know so many different groups of Jews all under one roof. Take advantage of it, learn a lot, and have a great and meaningful time!

Reconstructionist Judaism

Rabbi Jonathan B. Freirich
Reconstructionist Rabbinical College, 1999
Metro Director, Cleveland Hillels

Reconstructionism, in many ways, was made for Jews on campus. Reconstructionism is not just a movement, it is also a way of thinking about Judaism, and one way to sum up its central idea is to say that Judaism is for Jews. Similar to the notion of government "for the people, by the people," Reconstructionists think that Judaism should be determined by the needs and principles of those who participate. This means that Reconstructionists are very democratic. Even in congregations, big decisions are left up to the entire community to decide, not just a small group like a board. Also, Reconstructionist democracy is egalitarian and inclusive in many ways. Not only are women and men, including gay, lesbian, and bisexual individuals, considered to have equal shares in a community, but also everyone, from the community leaders to the people who only show up once in a while, has an equal vote. If you feel that you belong to the community, like Hillel on campus, then you have an equal stake in that community through your participation.

This is why Reconstructionism fits Judaism on campus so well: Hillel and other campus Jewish organizations offer resources for students interested in Judaism to explore their identities and activities in their own ways. Whether deciding how to keep kosher in the building, which prayer book to use in services, how many services, and which type to offer, or whether to go skiing or scuba diving, students make decisions for themselves. This is not to say that Reconstructionists don't take advantage of the wisdom of teachers and rabbis, but instead of telling Jews what to do, Reconstructionist leaders prefer to facilitate a conversation about how to do things and then work with the community to find a conclusion that everyone can agree on.

For example, a student who runs our Reform minyan once asked me about changing a part of the service. We discussed this and, to be honest, argued points of Jewish traditions and Reform traditions, and then I told the student that this is a student service, and he should talk with his peers and decide about the change with them. This is a good example of Reconstructionist thinking—lay out the issue, talk about our principles on the matter, talk about the relevant Jewish principles, and then work with the various participants to decide. The only thing I didn't do was ensure that everyone involved in organizing the service was also involved in learning about the background that I had worked on with the one student who wanted the change. Next time, I plan on holding a town meeting of some sort, so that more students have the opportunity both to learn and decide.

Reform Judaism

Rabbi Lisa L. Goldstein
Hebrew Union College–Jewish Institute of Religion, 1993
Executive Director, Hillel of San Diego

The fact that I grew up as a Reform Jew informs the way I think about Jewish campus life in a profound way. During my undergraduate years, the Reform group on campus was very weak; it seemed to me that Hillel was dominated by more traditionally observant Jews who had all gone to camp together and knew volumes more about Judaism than I did. I wanted to be a part of the

Jewish campus community, but I didn't feel that I fit in, and I didn't know how to carve out a place for myself. So I mostly stayed away.

Now that I am a Hillel director, I see that many Reform Jews feel the same way. They are proud of their background, but they don't always know what they want from Jewish life. Many Reform Jews have wonderful memories of UAHC camps and NFTY and still keep up with their friendships from there, but they aren't so sure how that translates into campus life. They also see how other students have different traditions and sometimes feel intimidated by that.

Perhaps the first step to deepen the Reform Jewish experience on campus needs to come from the Hillel staff in creating a safe space for Reform Jews. I believe it is important to have a Reform service available on Friday nights, where Reform Jews can explore the interplay between creative and traditional liturgy, Hebrew and English, guitar and other kinds of music. On my campus, this has created a core of over seventy Reform Jews who come to Shabbat every week. They know Hillel is a place for all kinds of religious connection—including theirs.

If, for some reason, Reform Jews do not feel they have adequate support from Hillel staff, all is not lost. The UAHC through Kesher has so many resources for Reform students—conference, materials, grant money. Part of becoming an adult is taking responsibility for one's own environment. Reform students have the opportunity to create their own community where Reform Judaism can flourish.

Once Reform Jews feel that they have a community of their own where they can be comfortable, they realize that the university is an ideal place to delve into the cornerstone of Reform Jewish integrity: learning! How do you know what aspects of Judaism are meaningful to you if you don't know very much about adult Judaism? The campus community is a perfect opportunity for Reform students to learn about Judaism from an independent perspective, to study texts, to try out new customs and rituals, to see what fits and what doesn't. What does the tradition say, and how do I feel about that? What is my own lived experience, and how can I incorporate that into belonging to a diverse community? What is compelling to me, and what makes me grow as a Jew and a human being?

College years are a wonderful opportunity to explore and question. I believe this is particularly important for Reform Jews, and as a Hillel rabbi I am delighted to work with these students in deepening their Jewish connections.

Name	e-mail	Phone number